my **revision** notes

Edexcel AS/A-level History

THE RISE AND FALL OF FASCISM IN ITALY c1911–46

Sarah Ward
Laura Gallagher

Series editor:
Peter Callaghan

Orders: please contact Bookpoint Ltd, 130 Milton Park, Abingdon, Oxon OX14 4SE. Telephone: +44 (0)1235 827720. Fax: +44 (0)1235 400454. Email education@bookpoint.co.uk Lines are open from 9 a.m. to 5 p.m., Monday to Saturday, with a 24-hour message answering service. You can also order through our website: www.hoddereducation.co.uk

ISBN: 978 1 4718 7652 3

First published in 2017 by

Hodder Education,
An Hachette UK Company
Carmelite House
50 Victoria Embankment
London EC4Y 0DZ
www.hoddereducation.co.uk

Impression number 10 9 8 7 6 5 4 3 2 1

Year 2020 2019 2018 2017

Illustrations by Integra
Typeset by Integra Software Services Pvt. Ltd., Pondicherry, India
Printed in Spain

A catalogue record for this title is available from the British Library.

My Revision Planner

REVISED

4 Challenges to, and the fall of, the Fascist State, c1935–46

REVISED

Introduction

About Paper 2

Paper 2 Option 2G.1: The rise and fall of fascism in Italy, c1911–46, is a depth study. Therefore it requires a detailed knowledge of the period that you are studying. Paper 2 tests you against two Assessment Objectives: AO1 and AO2:

AO1 tests your ability to:

- organise and communicate your own knowledge
- analyse and evaluate key features of the past
- make supported judgements
- deal with concepts of cause, consequence, change, continuity, similarity, difference and significance.

On Paper 2, AO1 tasks require you to write an essay from your own knowledge.

AO2 tests your ability to:

- analyse and evaluate source material from the past
- explore the value of source material by considering its historical context.

On Paper 2, the AO2 task requires you to write an essay which analyses two sources that come from the period you have studied.

At A-level, Paper 2 is worth 20 per cent of your qualification. At AS-level, Paper 2 is worth 40 per cent of your qualification. Significantly, your AS grade does not count towards your overall A-level grade. Therefore, you will have to take this paper at A-level in order to get the A-level qualification.

Structure

At AS and A-level, Paper 2 is structured around four key topics which cover the period 1894–1924.

The AS and A-level exams are divided into two sections. Section A tests your source analysis skills, whereas Section B tests your ability to write an essay from your own knowledge. Both sections focus on the four key topics. The question may deal with aspects of one of the topics, or may be set on issues that require knowledge of several or all of the topics.

The exam

At AS and A-level, the Paper 2 exam lasts for 1 hour and 30 minutes. It is divided into two sections, both of which test the depth of your historical knowledge. At AS-level, Section A (AO2) requires you to answer one compulsory question in two parts. Part (a) and Part (b) each refer to a different source. You should spend around 15 minutes on Part (a) and around 20 minutes on Part (b). You should also spend 15 to 20 minutes reading the sources and planning your answer. At A-level, Section A requires you to answer one compulsory question concerning two sources. You should spend 15 to 20 minutes reading the sources and planning your answer, and around 35 to 40 minutes writing the essay. At AS-level, Section B (AO1) requires you to write one essay from a choice of three. At A-level, Section B requires you to write one essay from a choice of two. The essays must be written from your own knowledge. As this is a depth paper, questions can be set on single events or single years. However, a question may cover more extended periods. You should aim to spend around 35 to 40 minutes writing the essay; this includes making a brief plan.

How to use this book

This book has been designed to help you to develop the knowledge and skills necessary to succeed in this exam. The book is divided into four sections – one for each of the key topics. Each section is made up of a series of topics organised into double-page spreads. On the left-hand page, you will find a summary of the key content you need to learn. Words in bold in the key content are defined in the glossary. On the right-hand page, you will find exam-focused activities. Together, these two strands of the book will take you through the knowledge and skills essential for exam success.

There are three levels of exam-focused activities.

- Band 1 activities are designed to develop the foundational skills needed to pass the exam.
- Band 2 activities are designed to build on the skills developed in Band 1 activities and to help you achieve a C grade.
- Band 3 activities are designed to enable you to access the highest grades.

Each section ends with an exam-style question and model high-level answer with commentary. This should give you guidance on what is required to achieve the top grades.

Examination activities

There are three levels of exam-focused activities:

- Band 1 activities are designed to develop the foundation skills needed to pass the exam. These have a green heading and this symbol: 
- Band 2 activities are designed to build on the skills developed in Band 1 activities and to help you to achieve a C grade. These have an orange heading and this symbol: 
- Band 3 activities are designed to enable you to access the highest grades. These have a purple heading and this symbol:

Some of the activities have answers or suggested answers on pages 101–103. These have the following symbol to indicate this: 

1 The Liberal State, c1911–18

Italy's political system

REVISED

In the early twentieth century, Italy was still a fairly new country. It had only been fully united in 1870, and its political system was created at that point. It was a parliamentary system similar to that in Britain, and the constitution was based on that of the formerly independent kingdom of Piedmont. This constitution was created in 1848, and was known as the *Statuto*. It guaranteed the following important rights:

- equality before the law
- the right of free assembly
- a free press.

It also set up the **constitutional monarchy** and elected parliament that became the basis of Italy's political system.

The Monarchy

Unlike in Britain, the King of Italy had wide-ranging political powers. He could:

- appoint and dismiss government ministers and senators, including the prime minister
- control foreign policy.

He was also the face of the government at times of crisis.

The Prime Minister

The Prime Minister was the head of the Government, and was responsible for the day-to-day running of the country. He needed the support of parliament to keep his position and to propose laws.

Parliament

There were two chambers in the Italian Parliament. The Senate was the upper house. Senators were appointed by the King for life. The Chamber of Deputies was the lower house. It was elected every five years and had more political power than the Senate. Government ministers were chosen from the Chamber of Deputies.

The electorate

The Chamber of Deputies was, in theory, democratically elected, but in reality only a small proportion of the Italian population could vote. There were limitations based on age, property ownership and educational qualifications. Until 1912, only 25 per cent of adult men could vote. This meant that most people did not participate in politics before 1912, meaning that many Italians felt alienated from the political system.

Political weaknesses

Apart from the political alienation felt by many Italians, the system was also very elitist, unstable and corrupt. Political parties did exist, but they acted more as labels for groups of ambitious men who wanted to gain power – they did not often have a coherent political ideology. As political parties were very weak, governments were always coalitions of different factions. This system of coalition-building became known as ***Trasformismo***. It meant Italian political life was very unstable, because coalitions fell apart quickly, leading to a succession of short-term governments. In the years 1900–11, for example, there were nine governments. Only one lasted more than two years.

Individual politicians often bribed political opponents, and those seeking to build a coalition would offer potential colleagues important jobs or financial incentives. Most of the Deputies were in parliament to serve local interests, and so they were not very attached to their party or faction. This meant they could be bribed to switch allegiance if they were offered enough money or a promotion. It also meant that there was little sense of national politics or unity in government.

As a consequence, the political system that resulted from unification seemed far removed from ordinary Italians' lives.

Political parties

Political parties operated as loose groupings rather than clearly defined organisations. The most important groupings were:

- Liberals
- Radicals and Republicans
- Socialists
- Catholics
- Nationalists.

Mind map

Use the information on the opposite page to add detail to the mind map below.

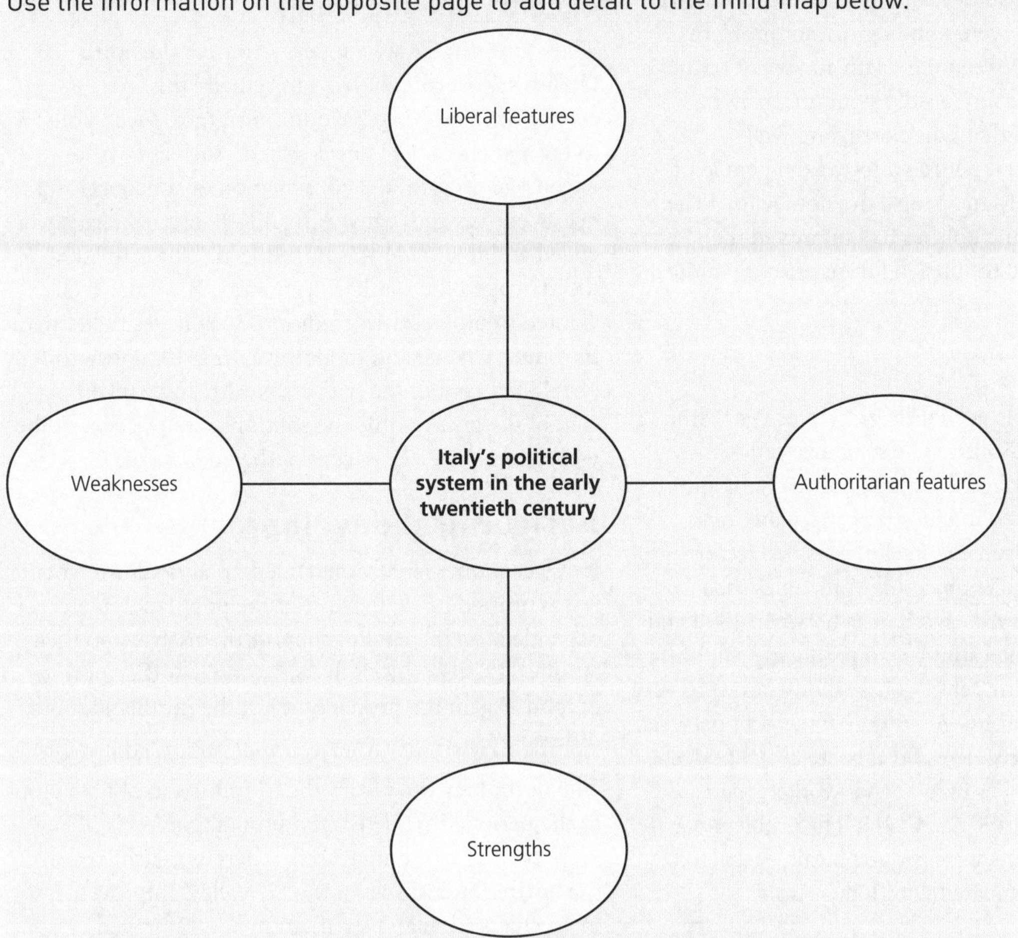

Spectrum of power

Below is a list of people or organisations that held power in Italy in this period. Use your own knowledge and the information on the opposite page to reach a judgement about the amount of power held by these people and organisations. Write numbers on the spectrum below to indicate their relative degrees of power. Having done this, write a brief justification of your placement, explaining why some of these people or organisations were more powerful than others.

1 The King

2 The Prime Minister

3 The Senate

4 The Chamber of Deputies

Less powerful ←——→ More powerful

Economic problems

REVISED

Italy's economy was still developing at the beginning of this period, but there were some significant problems that made a divide between the north and south of the country even more pronounced. Economic growth was concentrated mostly in the north, and well-intentioned agricultural policies affected the people of the south negatively. Many people did not feel that the government's economic policies had improved their lives, and this later led to support for increasingly radical political groups.

Industry

There was considerable economic growth under Prime Minister **Giovanni Giolitti**. The state invested in industries and encouraged the use of new technologies. Most of the growth was in industry, particularly **new industries**. Cheaper iron and steel imports led to the founding of motor and engineering companies such as Fiat, Isotta Fraschinin Alfa and Lancia between 1899 and 1906. Pirelli and Montecatini began producing sulphuric acid, rubber and electric cables. These industries were very profitable, and their profits grew by 10.6 per cent between 1896 and 1913. Exports increased at a rate of 4.5 per cent per year, and the number of industrial workers increased by 2 million between 1901 and 1911. The problem was that these developments were geographically restricted and of limited size compared with Italy's rivals.

Industrial development in the north

Industry was generally restricted to northern Italy, with only some developments elsewhere in Naples, Veneto and Tuscany and some sulphur mines in Sicily. The north-west specialised in engineering and textiles, the north produced chemicals, and steel and heavy machinery were produced in the north-east, in Sesto San Giovanni. The north-west was particularly successful because of its geographical closeness to the rest of Europe, its transport links, pre-existing industry, accessible markets and power sources.

However, even in the north development was not evenly spread. In 1911, Milan, Genoa and Turin accounted for 55 per cent of industrial income.

Italian industrial development was limited and localised for the following reasons:

- There was a need to import iron, steel and coal because of a lack of resources.
- Italy had a large but unskilled workforce.
- Industrial machinery needed to be imported.
- Communications, transport and energy sources were all underdeveloped in most areas.

Industry and the south

The south was far less modernised than the north. Giolitti's Government tried to remedy this. An economist, Francesco Saverio Nitti, introduced policies to try and encourage development, such as laws to encourage growth, the construction of aqueducts and tax incentives and loans. After 1900, internal tariffs were ended and free trade was introduced. Unfortunately, this damaged the southern economy, as southern elites wanted to protect their traditional privileges rather than introduce change and modernity. In 1910, northern Italy had 48 per cent of the nation's wealth and paid 40 per cent of the taxes, while the south had 27 per cent of the wealth and paid 32 per cent of the taxes.

Agricultural developments

Italy's economy largely depended on agriculture when it was unified in 1870. Most of the population were dependent on the land to support themselves and their families. Despite this, Italy was not self-sufficient in terms of food. Again the productivity of the north and south differed greatly.

The north benefited from the introduction of new crops in the period 1890–1910, and production levels of key crops such as wheat increased. There was rich land in the north, for example in the Po Valley. Improvements in mechanisation and fertilisation also improved productivity in the north, and irrigation and drainage systems protected farms from flooding. There were larger farms whose owners employed landless labourers when they needed them – and who sacked them when they did not. This was to lead to problems later in the period.

The south was not without its successful products. It produced some luxury items such as wine, oil and citrus fruits. On the whole though, the land was of poorer quality, partly due to deforestation. Disease and drought were regular occurrences in the summer, and a series of natural disasters from 1905 to 1908 damaged the economy. Government financial support was slow to arrive, making southerners believe that the northern politicians did not care about them.

Venn diagram

Use the information on the opposite page to complete the Venn diagram below, showing those economic features which were unique to the north, those which were unique to the south, and those which were common to both regions.

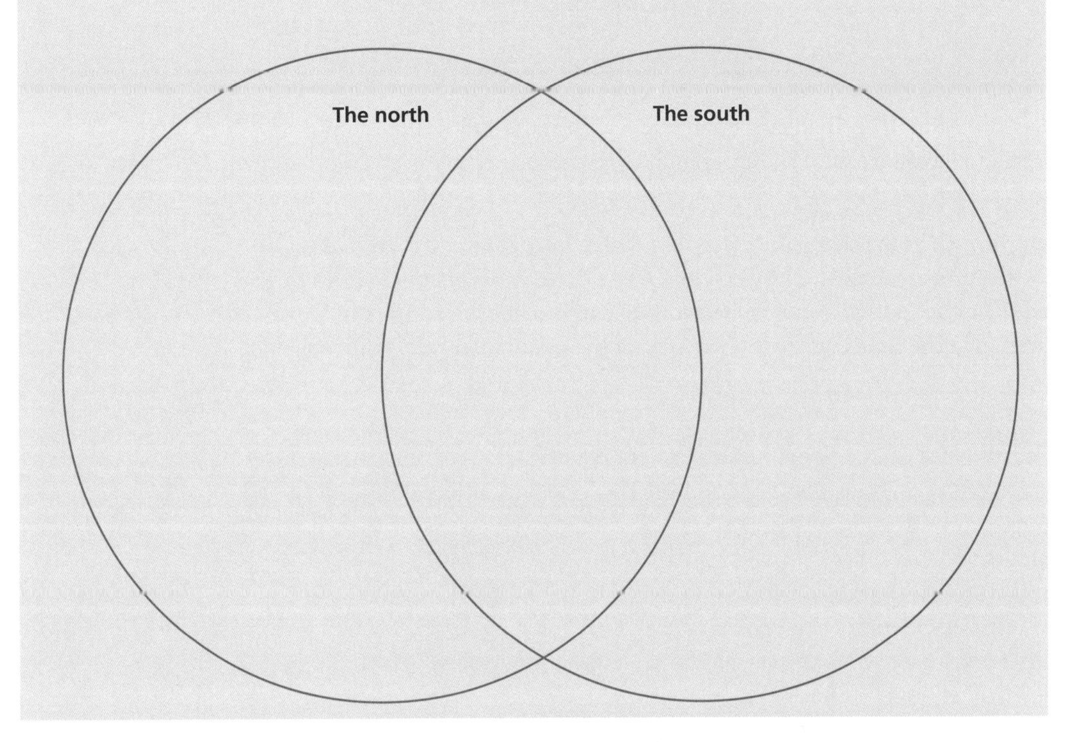

Develop the detail

Below is a sample exam question and a paragraph written in answer to this question. The paragraph contains a limited amount of detail. Annotate the paragraph to add additional detail to the answer.

How far were economic problems the main cause of social discontent in Italy in the period 1911–18?

Economic problems played some role in creating social discontent in Italy in the period 1911–18. Although many in the north benefited from industrial growth, southern workers suffered in this period. For example, Nitti's attempts to modernise southern industry were largely unsuccessful. In addition, there were significant problems with agriculture in the south. As a result of these problems, the south was significantly less wealthy than the north. In this way, economic problems contributed to social discontent in Italy in the period 1911–18 because they decreased standards of living for those in the south and accentuated the divide between the south and the north.

Social problems

REVISED

Italy had to contend with some serious social problems in the early twentieth century. Many of them were made worse by the economic weaknesses of the country. They included poverty, disease and illiteracy. In the south, the problems were even worse because of the weaker economy. There were landless labourers in both regions, and they were particularly vulnerable to poverty because they had no job security. When the landowner did not need them any more they went without work, and so they often struggled to feed their families.

Disease was a further problem often resulting from poverty. Diseases such as typhus, rickets and cholera were much more widespread in Italy than in many other European countries. Tuberculosis and malaria killed many people in the south, even until the 1930s. Poor living conditions made the spread of disease easier, and migration to the industrial towns meant that this problem only increased.

Literacy rates were very low when Italy was unified. More than 69 per cent of Italians were illiterate. As with the other problems, this was linked to poverty. The wealthy could afford to pay for private schools, and their children did not need to work to supplement the family's income. Again, illiteracy was higher in the south, where 80 per cent of the population were illiterate, and in the countryside.

Government efforts to address social problems

Giolitti's Government did try to improve the situation for Italy's poor. They introduced the following policies:

- sickness, accident and pension schemes
- raising the minimum working age to 12 years
- setting a maximum number of working hours
- placing responsibility for primary schooling on central government, which was more interested in increasing literacy than regional authorities
- reducing food taxes to make food more affordable
- passing laws to establish public holidays and provide free treatment for malaria.

Hospitals also improved in this period, meaning that more people were cured of illnesses and life expectancy increased. By 1914, Italians had the same life expectancy as other Europeans. By 1911, the national average for illiteracy was 37.6 per cent, and the number of schools had increased. Although illiteracy was still much higher in the south, the situation was improving.

Migration and emigration

One consequence of poverty and economic hardship was the desire of many Italians to improve their lives by either moving abroad or elsewhere within Italy. Thousands moved into towns to seek employment, although this was again largely limited to the northern cities.

Many other Italians sought a new life outside of Italy. This was a very risky strategy. The journey overseas could be hazardous and there was no guarantee of success. Despite this, approximately 200,000 Italians emigrated every year after the 1890s, and in 1912–13 alone around 1.5 million people left Italy – most of them from the south. This was viewed as a disaster for Italy, as people whose skills could have been used to strengthen Italy were leaving for the USA, South America and other places around the world.

Spot the mistake

Below are a sample exam question and a paragraph written in answer to this question. Why does this paragraph not get into Level 4? Once you have identified the mistake, rewrite the paragraph so that it displays the qualities of Level 4. The mark scheme on page 99 will help you.

How far is it accurate to describe Italy as 'unified' in the period 1911–18?

One way in which Italy could not be described as 'unified' in the period 1911–18 was in terms of education and literacy rates. There were significant differences in terms of social class and geography. For example, those who were richer could afford to send their children to private schools. In addition, those in the south were more likely to be illiterate. In this sense, Italy could not be described as 'unified' as some people were much better educated than others.

Spot the inference

High-level answers avoid excessive summarising or paraphrasing the sources. Instead they make inferences from the sources, as well as analysing their value in terms of their context. Below is a source and a series of statements. Read the source and decide which of the statements:

- make inferences from the source (I)
- paraphrase the source (P)
- summarise the source (S)
- cannot be justified from the source (X).

Statement	I	P	S	X
There was significant social and economic turmoil in Italy in this period.				
The writer of Source 1 believes that Giolitti's Government tried to make life easier for the poor.				
The writer of Source 1 believes that Italian governments in the period described did not deal effectively with the social and economic problems facing Italy.				
There were protests among labourers and peasants and those in the south.				
The writer of Source 1 believes that the main cause of social discontent was bad harvests.				
The writer of Source 1 believes that economic problems were a significant cause of social discontent.				
Politically, there were many twists and turns in Italy before the First World War.				

SOURCE 1

Adapted from Benito Mussolini, My Autobiography, *Paternoster Library, The Mayflower Press, 1928. Mussolini, at the time of writing in 1928, was dictator of Italy. In the following passage he is reflecting on politics just before the First World War.*

Those years before the World War were filled by political twists and turns. Italian life was not easy. Difficulties were many for the people. Our lack of political understanding brought at least one riot a week. During one government of Giolitti I remember 33 [riots]. They had their harvest of killed and wounded and of corroding bitterness of heart ... Riots and upheavals among day labourers, among the peasants in the Po Valley, riots in the south. And in the meantime, above all this wasting away of normal life, there went on the tournament and the joust of political parties struggling for power.

Giolitti's Government

REVISED

Giovanni Giolitti was one of the most important political figures in early twentieth-century Italy. He was involved in government for a long time, and was Prime Minister for most of the period 1903–14. Even when not Prime Minister he held other roles, such as Minister of the Interior. Giolitti was a skilled politician who was very good at forming the coalitions necessary for success in *Trasformismo*. He was a manipulator who was prepared to use bribery and the offer of promotions to achieve success. Yet he also had a vision of what he wanted Italy to be like: stronger, united, modernised. It led him to implement modernising policies and he was prepared to deal with a range of different political groups in order to achieve his aims.

Giolitti's reforms included policies related to welfare, literacy and economic prosperity. While they led to significant improvements in these areas, they did not help all of those whom they targeted. Industrial workers in particular became increasingly organised and joined organisations like unions to help achieve redress for their grievances. There were agricultural unions as well, such as the Federation of Agricultural Workers, founded in 1901. There were also Socialist unions and Catholic unions. Giolitti, instead of banning these organisations, tried to create reforms that brought these organisations and their members within the political process. He enacted measures to allow them to organise, protest and strike. He hoped that his welfare measures would bring more prosperity to the alienated workers and peasants and reduce their interest in striking.

These measures did not end worker grievances. The police supported the elites against the workers, sometimes violently repressing strikes. Economic production was still prioritised over worker grievances. As a result, workers continued to support the unions and parties they thought protected their interests. On the other hand, there were some wealthy and powerful Italians who thought Giolitti was not protecting their interests any more. They too sought other ways to achieve their goals, including supporting authoritarian parties or groups.

Giolitti and the Socialists

Giolitti targeted moderate Socialist Deputies to join his coalitions. The Socialists had been very successful in elections, with the Italian Socialist Party (PSI) winning about 20 per cent of the vote in 1909, and so it was important for Giolitti to try to include them. Those deputies who did collaborate with Giolitti were heavily criticised from within their own party. Apart from these deputies, the Socialists were never fully absorbed into Giolitti's coalitions. There were several reasons for this: police repression made it difficult for them to compromise with the state; the Socialists were divided; and the wider Socialist movement was much less prepared to engage with Giolitti than the politicians. Many Italian Socialists believed Giolitti's reforms were aimed at avoiding political instability rather than helping the people.

Giolitti and the Catholic Church

Giolitti was the first Liberal to appeal successfully to the Catholic vote. He saw Catholic support as a balance to the Socialists. The Catholic vote was potentially huge, and in the 1913 elections the Pope swung his support behind Giolitti. Giolitti was always wary of the Catholic alliance because he did not want to make promises that he could not deliver – such as the return of territory to the Vatican – and this meant the alliance was not a stable or permanent one.

Giolitti and the Nationalists

The first Nationalist party was set up in 1910, and by 1914 it had huge support. It was the movement most opposed to Giolitti's politics and methods. Nationalists hated Giolitti's foreign policy, and took advantage of a popular mood that bemoaned Italy's status in Europe, its lack of colonies, economic backwardness and defeat at Adowa (see page 76). They also appealed to middle-class Italians worried at Giolitti's concessions to the Socialists. They called for:

- a ban on public sector strikes
- stronger police powers
- protection for Italian industry from foreign competition
- a stronger army and more defence spending
- gaining the Italian-speaking territories of Trentino and Trieste from Austria
- colonial expansion.

Giolitti underestimated them as a threat due to their recent origin, but their opposition to his policies would have made them an unlikely coalition partner anyway.

Support or challenge?

Below is a sample exam question which asks how far you agree with a specific statement. Below this are a series of general statements which are relevant to the question. Using your own knowledge and the information on the opposite page, decide whether these statements support or challenge the statement in the question and tick the appropriate box.

'Giolitti's social and economic reforms in the early twentieth century were entirely ineffectual.' How far do you agree with this statement?

	Support	Challenge
The south remained poor and migration rates remained very high.		
The literacy rate increased dramatically.		
There was a significant difference between economic and social conditions in the north and those in the south.		
The police were not reformed and acted harshly against the workers.		
Fewer people died from disease and life expectancy increased.		
By 1914, Italians had the same life expectancy as other Europeans. Giolitti allowed workers to organise themselves into trade unions, but still saw economic production as more important than the issue of addressing worker grievances.		

Write the question (AS-level)

a

The following source relates to the situation in Italy before the First World War. Read the guidance detailing what you need to know about Italy during this period. Having done this, write an AS exam-style question using the source.

Why is Source 1 valuable to the historian for an enquiry into ...?

____

____

Explain your answer, using both the source, the information given about it and your own knowledge of the historical context.

SOURCE 1

Adapted from the writings of Antonio Gramsci, a former Socialist and a founder of the more radical Communist Party in 1921. In the following passage, written in the 1930s, Gramsci is analysing the leaders of the Liberal Party in the years up to 1914.

They [the Liberal leaders] said that they were aiming at the creation of a modern State in Italy, and they in fact produced a bastard. They aimed at stimulating the formation of an extensive and energetic ruling class, and they did not succeed; at integrating the people into the framework of the new State, and they did not succeed. The paltry political life ... the fundamental ... rebelliousness of the Italian popular classes, the narrow existence of a cowardly ruling stratum, they are all consequences of that failure.

Foreign policy in 1911: Italy and Libya

REVISED

In September 1911, Italy invaded Libya. There were several key reasons for the invasion:

- Italy wanted to assert colonial claims in North Africa in response to France's apparent efforts to expand in the region.
- Powerful Italian business interests pushed for the invasion after establishing investments in Libya.
- Popular opinion was strongly in favour of the invasion.
- Giolitti hoped that a successful Libyan war would weaken Nationalist support.

Events of the Libyan War

Italy declared war on the Ottoman Empire on 29 September 1911. Within three weeks, Italian forces had seized many of the ports and coastal towns, but found progress much harder after that point. The local Arabs saw the Italians as invaders rather than liberators, and so the Italian army had to fight both Turks and Arabs. Italy succeeded in gaining the Libyan territory she desired, but only through diplomatic pressure. She occupied 13 Turkish islands in the Aegean and because of Turkey's involvement in the **Balkan Wars** she was unable to resist for long. On 8 October 1912, the Turks formally surrendered Libya to Italy in the Treaty of Lausanne.

It was not quite the success it appeared for Italy, however, as the war was extremely costly. The Arabs continued to resist Italian control for many years, and so Italy had to keep large numbers of troops in Libya even after the end of the war. The war cost 1,300 million lire and 3,500 Italian troops were killed in the fighting.

Impact of the Libyan War

The Libyan War was not straightforwardly positive for Giolitti's Government. He could take credit for the military victory and the acquisition of Italy's first colony. On the other hand, the Nationalists claimed responsibility for pushing Giolitti into taking action. They gained popularity as a result. They also blamed Giolitti for the loss of life and the cost of the war, arguing that had it been managed properly Italy would have had even more success. It also led the Nationalists and Catholics into a temporary alliance and weakened the moderate Socialists. This meant that the Revolutionary Socialists took over the movement.

Another unexpected consequence was the extension of the **electoral franchise** in 1912 to all literate males over the age of 21 and all males regardless of education over the age of 30. This was an extension of Giolitti's pre-war reforms but was sped up by the war. Conscripted men were fighting overseas and it was proposed as a symbol of national unity that they be given the vote. It was also intended to bring more conservative rural voters to the polls, although it had the opposite effect, making government even more difficult.

Finally, the acquisition of Libya also had negative consequences:

- Libya produced the same crops as Italy, leading to a fall in Italian crop prices.
- Emigrants refused to move to Libya to start an Italian colony.
- The Ottoman Empire expelled 50,000 Italians in retaliation for the war, resulting in a loss of trade.

Add the context

Below is a sample A-level exam question with the accompanying sources. Having read the question and the sources, complete the following activity.

> How far could the historian make use of Sources 1 and 2 together to investigate the reasons for the Italian invasion of Libya in 1911?
>
> Explain your answer, using both sources, the information given about them and your own knowledge of the historical context.

First, look for aspects of the source that refer to the events and discussion that were going on around the time that the source was written. Underline the key phrases and write a brief description of the context in the margin next to the source. Draw an arrow from the key phrase to the context. Try and find three key phrases in each source.

Tip: look at the information above the source – you should contextualise this too. Don't forget to consider the date on which the source was written.

SOURCE 1

Adapted from the memoirs of Giovanni Giolitti, published in 1922.

We were forced, for unforeseen reasons, to disturb the peace in Europe. If we didn't go into Libya, another power would ... And Italy would not have tolerated this result for Libya; so we would have run the risk of a conflict with a European power, which would have been much more serious than a conflict with Turkey. Persisting in our situation, of having laid a claim on Libya to prevent others from going there without going there ourselves, would have been foolish, and would have created difficulties for us in all the other European questions.

SOURCE 2

From the writings of Gaetano Salvemini, published in 1914. Salvemini was a Socialist politician, historian and writer. He opposed the government of Giolitti. In 1911, he left the Socialist Party in protest at their 'silence and indifference' over the war.

Italy was bored in 1911. It was disgusted by everything. The democratic parties had hit rock bottom in public contempt. There was no man in sight to inspire confidence in a better future. Anything was better than universal stagnation. This "anything" was presented by the daily papers as the conquest of the "promised land": an easy conquest, nice and cheap, enormously productive, absolutely essential to Italy. So up with the war! Very soon the papers were overwhelmed by their readers' hysterical impatience: whoever told the biggest stories sold the greatest number of copies; as a result of such stories going from strength to strength, halfway through September there was no stopping the madness. Therefore, it became imperative for the government to decide on war straight away.

AS-level question

Why is Source 1 valuable to the historian for an enquiry into the reasons for the Italian invasion of Libya in 1911?

Explain your answer using the source, the information given about it and your own knowledge of the historical context.

Growing instability, 1912–14

REVISED

The period 1912–14 was one of growing political change and instability.

The growth of nationalism and socialism

Socialists and Nationalists became more critical of the Liberal-led government for different reasons. The Socialists thought the system was used to protect the elite and intimidate the working classes. Socialists argued that Italy's wealth was being wasted on foreign campaigns such as Libya. By 1913, the PSI was winning over 20 per cent of the total vote. The Nationalists were also becoming more powerful in this period. Drawing support from a mixture of business interests, journalists, poets and painters, the Italian National Association grew in strength. Nationalists believed the Liberals were failing to deal with the Socialist threat.

The impact of the franchise extension, 1912

The franchise was extended in 1912, partly because of the Libyan War (see page 14). The consequences of the franchise extension were not what Giolitti expected. He thought that it would lead to more votes from conservative voters and support from grateful Socialists.

In the 1913 elections, Giolitti's Liberals won fewer seats, declining from 370 to 318, but Giolitti still had a comfortable majority control of the Chamber of Deputies. He was able to form a coalition government with the support of the Catholic Union. The conservative peasants had given their votes to the Catholic party rather than the Liberals, meaning Giolitti was reliant on Catholic support. He was forced to make concessions such as making civil marriages precede a religious service. In turn, this meant that Radicals and Socialists would no longer collaborate with him.

Giolitti's resignation, 1914

By 1914, Giolitti was facing opposition from all sides. The Radicals withdrew support for his coalition government in February 1914 because of the concessions to the Catholics. This meant the collapse of the coalition. Giolitti resigned as Prime Minister on 21 March 1914. He remained a Deputy, and hoped to rebuild his reputation and make a successful return to government. In reality, his resignation was an event that was to prove the end of his 'system' and of *Trasformismo*. The new political parties were not loose groupings but were ideologically motivated and organised, unlike the Liberals and the politicians of the past.

After 1913, governments tended to be Nationalist, Catholic or both. The rise of a more aggressive form of politics coincided with the rising tensions internationally prior to the outbreak of the First World War in 1914.

The declaration of neutrality, 1914

In June 1914 the heir to the Austrian throne, Archduke Franz Ferdinand, was assassinated along with his wife while on a visit to Sarajevo. Their murder became a trigger for war in the tense political environment of Europe. The First World War broke out in August 1914 and Italy declared herself neutral. This continued Giolitti's policies and had been agreed in understandings with the **Entente Powers**. Giolitti led the movement for neutrality and remained committed to it. He spoke strongly in favour of neutrality in the Chamber of Deputies in December 1914. Giolitti, together with most Catholics and Socialists, as well as big business and most of the army, believed either that Italy was not ready for war or that war would be bad for the economy and Italian society.

Identify key terms

Below is an exam-style question which includes a key term or phrase. Key terms are important because their meaning can be helpful in structuring your answer, developing an argument and establishing criteria that will help form the basis of a judgement.

> 'Until 1914, the Liberal State was very successful.' How far do you agree with this statement?

- First, identify the key word or term. This will be a word or phrase that is important to the meaning of the question. Underline the word or phrase.
- Second, define the key phrase. Your definition should set out the key features of the phrase or word that you are defining.
- Third, make an essay plan that reflects your definition.
- Finally, write a sentence answering the question that refers back to the definition.

Now repeat the task, and consider how the change in key terms affects the structure, argument and final judgement of your essay.

> 'Until 1914, the Liberal State improved social and economic conditions in Italy.' How far do you agree with this statement?

Support your judgement

Below is an exam-style question and two basic judgements. Read the exam question and the two judgements. Support the judgement that you agree with most strongly by adding a reason that justifies the judgement.

> 'Until 1914, the Liberal State was very successful.' How far do you agree with this statement?

Overall, until 1914, the Liberal State was essentially successful in the sense that ...

____

____

Overall, until 1914, the Liberal State was not successful in the sense that ...

____

____

Tip: in order to reach a judgement about the level of success of the Liberal State in this period, consider how far it met its own aims.

Tip: whichever option you choose you will have to weigh up both sides of the argument. You could use words such as 'whereas' or 'although' in order to help the process of evaluation.

The impact of the First World War, part 1

REVISED

The intervention crisis, 1914–15

At the outbreak of war, most Italians were against military intervention on either side. As the war continued, however, opinions changed. By 1915, the question revolved around which side to support rather than whether to remain neutral.

Reasons for supporting neutrality

Those who supported entry into the war in 1914 were a minority.

- An alliance with Germany and Austria–Hungary was unattractive because of the Italian aim of regaining territory from Austria–Hungary.
- Neutrality was seen as a better choice economically and militarily.
- The Catholics and the political parties of the left opposed intervention. Many wanted to prioritise domestic issues rather than war.

The shift towards intervention

There are a variety of reasons why Italian popular support moved towards supporting intervention between August 1914 and May 1915, the point at which Italy joined the war.

- The Nationalist movement began campaigning for intervention in favour of the Entente Powers instead of the **Central Powers** as it was hoped that Italy could expand its territory that way.
- The Nationalists used the press to popularise their views. Allied propaganda also supported them. The former Socialist journalist **Benito Mussolini** and the poet and Nationalist **Gabriele D'Annunzio** were vocal in their support.
- The police and military supported intervention by encouraging pro-intervention demonstrations and breaking up those arranged to protest against it.

The Treaty of London, 1915

The Prime Minister, Antonio Salandra, was in favour of a treaty with the Entente Powers because of the potential to make large territorial gains. He began negotiations with both sides in the war; the Entente Powers made more promises in terms of territory, while Austria–Hungary declared she would not give Trentino to Italy in exchange for military support. Britain and France promised a range of territories, such as Austrian lands in the southern Tyrol. The Treaty of London was negotiated in secret by Salandra and **King Victor Emmanuel III**, and parliament was forced to accept it, despite the lack of consultation involved.

The Treaty of London was signed on 26 April 1915 and included a number of significant promises, including territorial gains and a share in any future war **reparations**. As a result, Italy entered the war on the side of the Entente Powers in May 1915.

Select the detail

Below is a sample exam A-level question with the accompanying sources. Having read the question and the sources, complete the following activity.

How far could the historian make use of Sources 1 and 2 together to investigate the reasons why Italy entered the First World War in 1915 on the side of the Entente Powers?

Below are three claims that you could make when answering the question. Read the claims and then select quotes from the sources to support them. Copy down the quotes in the space provided.

Tip: keep the quotes short; never copy more than a sentence. Remember, sometimes a few words embedded in a sentence is all you need to support your claims.

Source 1 is useful because it shows how the Italian Prime Minister justified entering the war on the side of the Entente Powers.

Both sources are useful because they contain evidence that Italian public opinion was in favour of joining the war on the side of the Entente Powers.

Source 2 is useful because it suggests reasons why the Italian people supported joining the war on the side of the Entente Powers.

SOURCE 1

From a speech by Prime Minister Antonio Salandra to the Italian nation on 23 May 1915, announcing Italy's entrance into the First World War. From David Evans, Years of Liberalism and Fascism: Italy 1870–1945, *p.40.*

I address myself to Italy and the civilised world in order to show not by violent words but by exact facts and documents, how the fury of our enemies has vainly attempted to diminish the high moral and political dignity of the cause which our arms will make prevail ... The horrible crime of Sarajevo was exploited as a pretext a month after it happened – this was proved by the refusal of Austria to accept the very extensive attitudes of Serbia ... The truth is that Austria and Germany believed until the last day that they had to deal with an Italy, weak, blistering, but not capable of ... enforcing by arms her good right ... In the blaze thus kindled internal discussions melted away and the whole nation was joined in a wonderful moral union, which will prove our greatest source of strength in the severe struggle that faces us.

SOURCE 2

An extract from the memoirs of the English ambassador to Italy, Sir James Rennell Rodd, giving his explanation of Italy's reasons for supporting the Entente Powers.

I have sometimes been asked by my countrymen how far I was responsible for the entry of Italy into the war. Such a question reveals, I think, a rather insular misapprehension of what really took place in Italy ... I have never doubted and have constantly affirmed both at the time and since that the moving impulse which drew the people together and led them to unite with the Allies against the forces of aggression was in the main that elemental love of justice which is in their nature. Every act committed by the enemy which estranged the sense of a common humanity had added strength to the movement, and the final rupture with the Central Powers came to them as a welcome relief.

The impact of the First World War, part 2

REVISED

Military stalemate

Problems began to emerge soon after Italy's entry into the war in May 1915, and a military stalemate quickly developed:

- Italy was unprepared for the war. Many of its best soldiers were in Libya, the mobilisation of troops was disorganised and there were serious shortages of arms and munitions.
- General Cadorna pursued a strategy of massed infantry attacks against entrenched positions. In the first two advances in 1915, 62,000 men were killed and 170,000 injured without any notable change in the military situation.

Austria's first major offensive in northern Italy took place in 1916. It was contained by the Italian army but the scale of the threat caused discontent in both the army and government, and it caused the fall of Salandra's Government.

Defeat at Caporetto, October 1917

In October 1917, Austrian and German forces mounted a sudden attack at Caporetto. They shelled the Italian artillery and used gas against their opponents. Italy's response was chaotic. Two hundred thousand soldiers lost contact with their regiments, and thousands of troops streamed down from the hills in a frenzy of confusion.

Cadorna blamed the defeat on cowardice, and had several thousand soldiers executed. The Government responded by removing Cadorna, replacing him with General Diaz.

Socialist responses to the war

The Socialists had been opposed to the war from the outset. The PSI was committed to peace, and gained growing support from opponents of the war. However, many Socialists became involved in the war effort, establishing local councils to organise rations and welfare, and co-operatives to prevent profiteering. Trade unions helped to safeguard jobs, wage rises and worker exemption from military service. Their opponents claimed that the Socialists were responsible for sabotaging the war effort, ignoring the fact that industrialists were making huge profits from the war.

Some Socialists did stay aloof from the war, and socialism as a movement became more divided in the war years. The Russian Revolution of 1917 sparked a new wave of unrest and the Socialist Party tried to use this as a model of change for Italy. These messages appealed to the workers but not to the army, who remained unsympathetic to the workers.

The war economy and the cost of war

The armed forces had begun the war with limited equipment and supplies, and the economy was unprepared for war. By 1918, this deficit had been made up. Italy had more cannons in the field than Britain, had created an aircraft industry, and the company Fiat became the leading manufacturer of trucks and lorries in Europe. This was achieved by a strategy of 'production at all costs'. The state bought whatever industry could produce at whatever price. Industrialists were celebrated and amassed huge personal fortunes.

Workers were placed under military discipline during the war. They could not change jobs or take strike action, and the working week was increased. Discontent among the workers led to increased support for the Socialist parties.

Peasant soldiers were promised that they would be granted land at the end of the war. Millions of men returned to the countryside in 1918–19, but the promised land reform did not materialise.

The war economy had serious consequences after the war, including:

- an enormous government budget deficit
- a huge rise in the national debt
- debts of more than 15 billion lire to Britain and 8.5 billion to the USA
- inflation, large price rises and significant economic instability after the government printed money when it realised it could borrow no more.

The economy was still short of natural resources, exports were low and the consumer market was weak. All of these factors would make economic recovery after the war extremely hard.

Identify the concept

a

Below are five sample exam questions based on some of the following concepts:

- Cause questions concern the reasons for something, or why something happened.
- Consequence questions concern the impact of an event, an action or a policy.
- Change/continuity questions ask you to investigate the extent to which things changed or stayed the same.
- Similarity/difference questions ask you to investigate the extent to which two events, actions or policies were similar.
- Significance questions concern the importance of an event, an action or a policy.

Read each of the questions and work out which of the concepts they are based on.

How far did the lives of poor Italians change in the period 1911–18? (AS question)

'The First World War had only negative consequences for the people of Italy.' How far do you agree?

'The Liberal State transformed Italy in the period 1911–18.' How far do you agree?

How far was dislike of *Trasformismo* the most important factor in Italy's political changes from 1911 to 1914? (AS question)

'The most important cause of the fall of Giolitti was the war in Libya.' How far do you agree with this statement?

How far was the signing of the Treaty of London the most important turning point in the intervention crisis of 1914–15?

Add the context

Below is a sample AS exam question with the accompanying source. Having read the question and the source, complete the following activity.

How much weight do you give the evidence of Source 1 for an enquiry into the reasons for the Italian defeat at Caporetto in 1917?

First, look for aspects of the source that refer to the events and discussion that were going on around the time that the source was written. Underline the key phrases and write a brief description of the context in the margin next to the source. Draw an arrow from the key phrase to the context. Try and find three key phrases in the source.

Tip: your contextual knowledge may not always support the information in the source. You could also consider ways in which your knowledge of context can be used to challenge the account of the source. In cases such as these, consider how the provenance of the source may have had an impact on its accuracy.

SOURCE 1

From Luigi Cadorna's official statement following the Italian defeat at Caporetto, dated 28 October 1917. Cadorna was the Italian Chief of Staff from 1914 until 1917. He was sacked shortly after the Battle of Caporetto.

A violent attack and the feeble resistance of detachments of the Second Army permitted Austro-German forces to pierce our left wing on the Julian front.

The valiant efforts of other troops were not successful in preventing the enemy from penetrating to the sacred soil of our Fatherland.

The bravery displayed by our soldiers in so many memorable battles fought and won in the past two and a half years gives our Supreme Command a pledge that this time, too, the army to which the honour and safety of the country are entrusted will know how to fulfil its duty.

The significance of victory

REVISED

General Diaz introduced a number of reforms to improve both morale and the military situation. Rations were improved, troops were given more days' leave and a servicemen's association was established to look after the welfare of troops and their families. Diaz was far more cautious in battle than Cadorna had been, and lost fewer men in action.

The military situation stabilised in 1918, when Austria–Hungary and Germany were struggling. In October 1918, German forces were in retreat after a concerned attack by Entente forces, and the Italian army attacked Austro-Hungarian forces near the site of the battle of Caporetto. The battle of Vittorio Veneto resulted in the collapse of the Austro-Hungarian front in Italy. The Italians took 500,000 prisoners of war and the defeat caused the Austrians to seek peace. An armistice was signed in November 1918.

Italy had lost approximately 700,000 men and made enormous economic sacrifices for the war effort. In return she gained territory, a sense of unity and national pride – but this was only in the short term.

Italy and the peace settlement of 1919–20

In 1915, the Treaty of London had promised Italy substantial territorial gains from the Austrian and Ottoman empires. At the peace settlement of 1919–20, Italy gained Trentino, South Tyrol and Istria from Austria–Hungary, along with part of Dalmatia and the port of Trieste. The Prime Minister, Vittorio Orlando, had expected to gain the port of Fiume, the whole of Dalmatia and a number of colonial territories. He left the peace conference in disgust. Italian Nationalists saw the peace as a betrayal of the country's efforts during the war, and regarded the settlement as a '**mutilated victory**'. The peace settlement was a significant factor in causing post-war instability in Italy.

Complete the graph

Use the information on the opposite page to complete the graph below.

1. Along the *x*-axis plot the key events of Italy's involvement in the First World War.
2. Reach a judgement about the level of success of Italy's war effort at each point.
3. Place a mark on the graph to indicate the level of success at each key event. For example, if you feel Italy's war effort was extremely successful, place your mark at the top of the graph.
4. Once you have plotted marks for each key event, draw a line joining these marks. This line should give you an overview of Italy's experiences during the war.

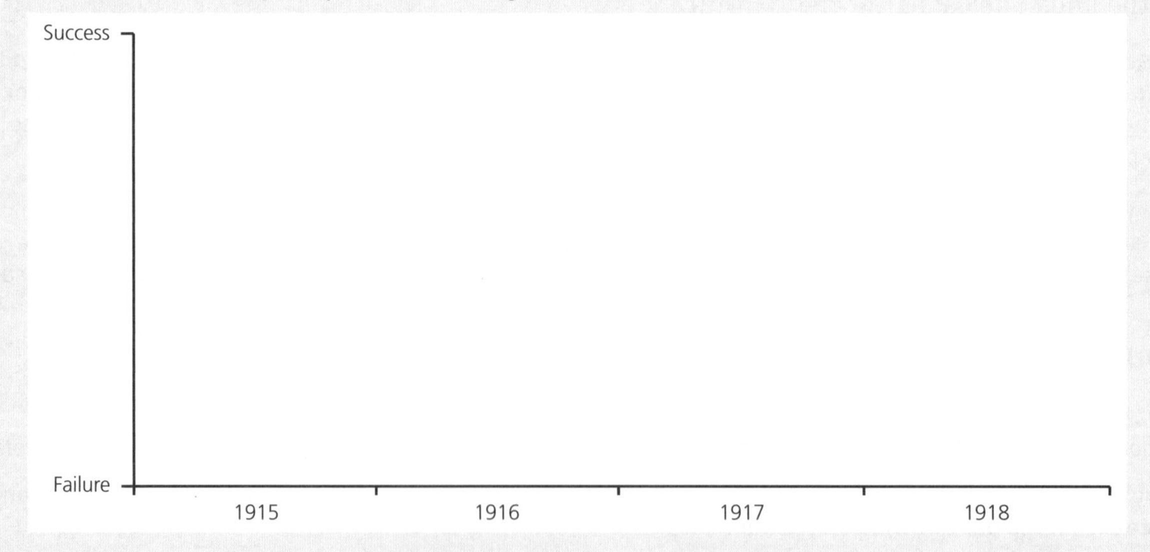

Recommended reading

- R. Absolom, *Italy Since 1800: A Nation in the Balance?*, Chapter 3 (1995).
- M. Clark, *Modern Italy, 1871–1995*, Chapter 5 (1996).
- A. de Grand, *Italian Fascism: Its Origins and Development*, 3rd ed., Chapter 1 (2000).

Exam focus (AS-level)

REVISED

Below is an AS exam-style question and model answer. Read it and the comments around it.

Part (a)

Why is Source 1 valuable to the historian for an enquiry into Italian attitudes to the Central Powers in 1915?

SOURCE 1

From a speech by Prime Minister Antonio Salandra to the Italian nation on 23 May 1915, announcing Italy's entrance into the First World War on the side of the Entente Powers. From David Evans, Years of Liberalism and Fascism: Italy 1870–1945, *page 40.*

'I address myself to Italy and the civilised world in order to show not by violent words but by exact facts and documents, how the fury of our enemies has vainly attempted to diminish the high moral and political dignity of the cause which our arms will make prevail ... The horrible crime of Sarajevo was exploited as a pretext a month after it happened – this was proved by the refusal of Austria to accept the very extensive attitudes of Serbia ... if there had been a possibility of mediation being exercised, it would not have interrupted hostilities which had already begun ... The truth is that Austria and Germany believed until the last day that they had to deal with an Italy, weak, blistering, but not capable of ... enforcing by arms her good right ... In the blaze thus kindled internal discussions melted away and the whole nation was joined in a wonderful moral union, which will prove our greatest source of strength in the severe struggle that faces us'.

This source is valuable for an enquiry into Italian attitudes to the Central Powers in 1915 because it is from a speech by Antonio Salandra, the Prime Minister of Italy from March 1914 to spring 1916, who provides the official political position of the Italian Government and was involved in the discussions prior to the decision to enter the war. Secondly, it gives a sense of the way that Italy's decision had changed from her initially neutral stance. Finally, the source is informative as to the language of nationalism that had become prominent in Italian politics.

This is a focused introduction that outlines the structure of the rest of the essay.

The speech was given by Salandra. He was deeply involved in Italy's negotiations with other powers regarding entry into the First World War. He had worried that Giolitti's decision to declare neutrality meant that Italy would not benefit from future peace negotiations, and that Italy would be seen as less important within Europe. This source is useful because he had a detailed understanding of the reasons behind the new decision to enter the war on the side of the Entente Powers, therefore, and had experienced the negotiations both with other powers and within government.

The essay uses detailed knowledge of the historical context to make inferences about the usefulness of the source.

Here the answer explains and makes a reasoned inference from a key phrase in the source, which is related directly to the question.

The speech is also useful for understanding Italian attitudes to the Central Powers because it demonstrates how the Italian Government's position had changed since 1913. The fact that Italy was not notified by Austria of the ultimatum being sent to Serbia on 28 June 1914 meant she was released from her Triple Alliance obligations, and so could make her own decision regarding intervention. In the speech Salandra particularly focuses on Austria and the ultimatum, partly because this aggressive action could be seen as humiliating to Italy, but also because Austria-Hungary had refused to cede territory such as Trentino in return for Italian support in the war. The decision to support the Entente Powers was influenced by their agreement to hand over territory to Italy, hence the decision to ally with Britain, France and Russia.

Here the answer selects aspects of the source which support the point being made. It also explains the meaning and significance of the quote in its historical context.

Finally the speech was written at a time when nationalism was rising as a political force. In this speech Salandra uses Nationalist language to refer to the Austrian and German attitudes to Italy. Although the first Nationalist party had only been founded in 1910, it became rapidly very successful, and the Nationalists strongly supported intervention. This speech, therefore, appeals to Nationalist opinion when it refers to Austria and Germany's belief that Italy was weak and unable to fight, as well as the 'moral union' of the nation. This demonstrates the importance of nationalism within Italian politics and its usefulness as a way for the government to persuade the Italian people of the reasons behind its decision.

In conclusion, there is much of value in the source for an enquiry into Italian attitudes to the Central Powers because of the importance of its author in making the decision, for what it can say about changing attitudes to the Central Powers and regarding the influence of nationalism in Italy at the time.

This response has a strong focus upon the question and gives three clear reasons why the source is useful for the enquiry. Passages from the source, a consideration of the source's context and the nature, origin and purpose of the source are used to make valid inferences.

Part (b)

How much weight do you give the evidence of Source 1 for an enquiry into Italian attitudes to the Central Powers in 1915?

The source clearly has some value for an enquiry into Italian attitudes to the Central Powers in 1915. Salandra was heavily involved in the negotiations for entry into the First World War and so his arguments about the actions of the Central Powers are useful. Despite this, Salandra does not mention the negotiations regarding territorial gains for Italy, and is attempting in this source to gain the support of the Italian people for intervention in favour of the Entente Powers. This clearly limits the value of the source.

This is a focused introduction that sets out a range of ways in which the source can be used.

The speech in Source 1 was given in 1915 by Salandra while Prime Minister of Italy. Although its purpose is to persuade and to present an official government line, and it neglects to mention the negotiations, this does not mean the source should be dismissed. Indeed, Italy had been angry about the Austrian failure to inform her about the Serbian ultimatum since 28 June 1914, and so the argument that this was a primary reason for siding against the Central Powers is persuasive as a partial explanation. It had been a focus of interventionist arguments in favour of joining the war, and Salandra was one politician who had long been doubtful about Giolitti's neutral stance from 1913 onwards.

Here the essay uses knowledge of the historical context to evaluate the usefulness of Salandra's comments on Italy's entry into the First World War.

Despite this, Salandra's argument that the Serbian ultimatum was the prime reason for the intervention is not entirely convincing, neither is the argument that the Central Powers should be opposed because of their view of Italy. Indeed, the entire question of territorial negotiations with both sets of powers is entirely avoided, or cloaked in Nationalist language. Italy's allegiance was secured by the Entente Powers after the Central Powers refused to promise Italy more land in potential peace negotiations, and this is not mentioned at all in the source. Salandra was deeply involved in the negotiations, and so the decision not to discuss them in

Salandra's argument that the Serbian ultimatum was the main reason for intervention is evaluated in terms of the historical context.

the speech can only have been deliberate. It is plausible to infer that this would not have been a noble or honourable way to present the decision to enter the war. The idea of an affronted Italy that needed to fight to regain her honour appealed to Nationalists, and was calculated to rouse the population in favour of the war.

In conclusion, the source is partially useful as it is likely to be accurate about the view of the Austrian ultimatum in 1914, and shows the importance of appealing to Nationalists. On the other hand, it omits one of the most important reasons why Italy fought against the Central Powers in the First World War, and so is clearly limited in some important respects.

The overall value of the source is evaluated in terms of valid criteria. The conclusion distinguishes between different ways in which the source can be used.

This answer maintains a strong focus on the question. It discusses a number of ways in which the source can be used, and notes the limitations of the source by using contextual knowledge.

Support or challenge?

Below is a sample exam question which asks how far you agree with a specific statement. Below this are a series of general statements which are relevant to the question. Using your own knowledge and the information in this chapter to decide whether these statements support or challenge the statement in the question and tick the appropriate box.

How far do you agree that Giolitti's government provided Italy with political stability in the years 1903–14?

	Support	Challenge
Trasformismo and coalition governments		
Giolitti and trade unions		
Attitude of the PSI towards the government		
Giolitti and the Catholic Church		
The growth of the Nationalists		

2 The rise of Mussolini and the creation of a Fascist dictatorship, 1919–26

Challenges to the Liberal State

REVISED

The 'mutilated victory'

Italy was very successful in the peace negotiations after the First World War. It achieved most of the territorial gains promised in the Treaty of London (see page 22) and was granted 14,500 square kilometres of land. This was more than any other victorious European country. Despite this, many Italians were dissatisfied with the peace settlement. They believed that all of the territorial aspects of the Treaty of London should have been granted. The most controversial Italian demands, however, were not even in the Treaty of London – demands for the Brenner Pass between Italy and Austria and for the port of Fiume.

Italy received Trentino, Trieste, Istria, the Brenner and some territories not in the Treaty of London, such as some of the Dalmatian Islands. Italy was also allowed to receive German war reparations and was given a permanent seat in the newly formed **League of Nations**.

Italian feelings of betrayal remained, however, and Fiume became a powerful symbol of their discontent. It was exploited by Italian Nationalists and Fascists to emphasise the betrayal of the Italian armed forces by both the **Allies** and a weak Liberal government. The phrase 'mutilated victory' was used by Italian Nationalists to describe the perceived mistreatment of Italy by the Allies.

The occupation of Fiume

In 1919, the Italian Prime Minister, Vittorio Orlando, raised the issue of Fiume with the Allied leaders. Britain and the USA felt that Fiume should remain part of the newly created nation of Yugoslavia. Before 1919, Fiume was part of the Austro-Hungarian Empire and had a mixed population of Croats and Italians. It had not formed part of the Treaty of London negotiations. Nationalists wanted Fiume because its 50 per cent Italian-speaking population meant that, for them, it was 'Italian'. The Allies rejected Italy's request, and the negotiators were seen as failures for not achieving the demand, no matter how weak the basis was for the demand in terms of previous agreements.

This failure led to the poet and Nationalist Gabriele D'Annunzio leading an invasion and seizure of Fiume in September 1919.

Events of the occupation of Fiume

In September 1919, D'Annunzio, alongside Nationalists, army officers and industrialists, led a coup to seize Fiume. He led 2,000 former solders, known as *arditi*, and seized control of Fiume, calling it the Free State of Fiume. Allied troops withdrew and did not resist the takeover. The occupation lasted 15 months.

During the occupation, Nationalists of all types flocked to the city, which had a festive atmosphere. D'Annunzio made long speeches and introduced many elements of later Fascist regimes, for example:

- the militia
- the 'Roman salute'
- the castor oil punishment for those who opposed them
- the title of *Duce* (leader)
- black shirts for those who supported the movement
- flamboyant rhetorical public speeches.

Meanwhile, Giovanni Giolitti opened negotiations with Yugoslavia, reaching an agreement in November 1920. The agreement was called the Treaty of Rapallo and declared Fiume an independent city. This was generally welcomed in Italy, where many had tired of D'Annunzio's antics. In December, Giolitti's new Government sent in the Italian army and navy to remove D'Annunzio.

Significance of the occupation

Many Italians were critical of Giolitti's actions, seeing them as unpatriotic. The occupation became a symbol of Nationalist defiance, and the Government's reluctance to act and the slow speed with which it intervened damaged its credibility. Their unwillingness to prevent such illegal actions by Nationalist or Fascist groups gave their opponents more momentum, revealing that force could be used to achieve political aims. D'Annunzio's actions influenced Mussolini and the Fascist movement in Italy. More Italians became attracted to the political extremes.

Identify an argument

a

Below are a series of definitions, a sample exam question and two sample conclusions. One of the conclusions achieves a high mark because it contains an argument. The other achieves a lower mark because it contains only description and assertion. Identify which is which. The mark scheme on page 99 will help you.

- Description: a detailed account.
- Assertion: a statement of fact or an opinion which is not supported by a reason.
- Reason: a statement which explains or justifies something.
- Argument: an assertion justified with a reason.

How far does Italy's 'mutilated victory' after the First World War account for increasing dissatisfaction with the Liberal Government in Italy in the period 1918–22?

Overall, Italy's 'mutilated victory' played a key role in accounting for increasing dissatisfaction with the Liberal Government in Italy in the period 1918–22. Many Italians were unhappy with the terms of the peace treaty and believed that the Liberal Government had failed to ensure that Italy was justly rewarded for its role in the war. Consequently, while other factors, such as economic problems and social problems, heightened tensions, the impact of the 'mutilated victory' was most important because it created the impression that the Italian Government was not acting in the interests of the Italian people.

Overall, Italy's 'mutilated victory' played a role in accounting for increasing dissatisfaction with the Liberal Government in Italy in the period 1918–22. The terms of the peace treaty did not reflect all of the demands made by Italy in the Treaty of London, and many people were disappointed with the peace settlement. However, the terms of the peace treaty did grant Italy more land than any other victorious European nation, with Italy receiving Trentino, Trieste, Istria, the Brenner and other additional territories.

Eliminate irrelevance

a

Below are a sample exam question and a paragraph written in answer to this question. Read the paragraph and identify parts of the paragraph that are not directly relevant to the question. Draw a line through the information that is irrelevant and justify your deletions in the margin.

How far do you agree that the invasion of Fiume was the main reason for the political instability of the Liberal State in the years 1918–22?

The invasion of Fiume in September 1919 played a key role in undermining the Liberal State in the years 1918–22. In this respect, the invasion was significant for three reasons. Firstly, the invasion showed the lack of support for the Government among the military. The invasion, which involved two thousand soldiers, occurred in defiance of the Liberal Government, and indicated that many in the military were not loyal to the Government. This had also been a problem in 1916, when many soldiers had expressed discontent at Italy's Government during the war. Secondly, the invasion showed the lack of popular support for the Liberal Government. Many in Italy supported the invasion, and viewed D'Annunzio as a hero. D'Annunzio was also famous for being a poet. Thirdly, the invasion demonstrated the power of force, undermining the Liberal State's reliance on compromise and negotiation. In this way, the invasion of Fiume contributed to the political instability of the Liberal State in the years 1918–22 by emphasising the level of popular dissatisfaction with the Liberal Government and its methods.

Post-war economic crisis

REVISED

Italy faced severe economic problems in the years 1919–22, largely because of its involvement in the First World War. Inflation had a huge impact on the cost of living, particularly in urban areas. Businesses were affected when military contracts were stopped. This, in turn, caused rising unemployment. By 1919, 2 million Italians were unemployed. The savings of the middle classes were badly damaged and they became even more disillusioned with the Government. All social groups affected by the economic problems searched for solutions, and in doing so they became more willing to turn to the political extremes.

Rural areas

Returning soldiers forcibly occupied lands in southern Italy, and the number of peasant landowners increased dramatically. They had profited from the war enough to be able to buy the land they farmed, because wartime food price inflation meant that they made more money from the food they sold.

Some left-wing groups tried to solve these problems with labour-owned collective farms. In other areas, local government was run by the Socialists, who set local wage rates and working conditions. In 1919 and 1920, Giolitti's coalition Government ordered **prefects** to legalise land confiscations. All of these developments made landlords and large tenant farmers feel more threatened.

Social discontent

Economic problems help to explain the increase in militancy among urban workers after 1918. This included a huge increase in strikes in 1919–20, known as the *Biennio Rosso* or 'Two Red Years'. In 1919, for example, there were 1,663 strikes in industry and 208 in agriculture. In September 1920, the 'occupation of the factories' took place in which 400,000 workers took over their factories. Increasing numbers of workers and peasants were involved in these actions, while membership of workers' organisations also grew rapidly.

Another sign of discontent at the economic problems was food riots. These riots, caused by a sharp increase in food prices, broke out spontaneously in June 1919. The Government ordered local authorities to set up food committees to requisition food and issued price decrees to halve the price of foodstuffs.

Some Socialists called for a Communist revolution like that in Russia, though this was never a serious threat. Despite this, the pressure of the strikes and increasing Socialist support led the Government to make some significant concessions, for example it:

- introduced a minimum wage
- established an eight-hour working day
- officially recognised factory grievance committees.

Discontent among the elites and middle classes

The reforms and initiatives above caused discontent among wealthier people. Industrialists feared a loss of influence as well as a takeover of the country by the Socialist movement. They felt that the elites should have power rather than the lower classes. This led them to amplify the 'red threat' more than it probably deserved.

The middle classes and **petty bourgeoisie** were also disenchanted. They were hit hard by the economic problems and often did not have unions to represent their interests. Due to inflation, their savings had lost value and they saw the industrial workers gaining economically at their expense. There was extra tax pressure on the middle class. Their frustrations were aimed at the Government, and they too looked for answers in the political extremes. They formed associations to represent their economic interests against those of big business and the working class.

These upper and middle class groups began to turn to fascism in the belief that Fascist groups would protect their economic, social and political interests.

Spot the inference

a

High-level answers avoid excessive summarising or paraphrasing the sources. Instead they make inferences from the sources, as well as analysing their value in terms of their context. Below is a source and a series of statements. Read the source and decide which of the statements:

- make inferences from the source (I)
- paraphrase the source (P)
- summarise the source (S)
- cannot be justified from the source (X).

Statement	I	P	S	X
The gangs in Italy carried out pickpocketing, abuse, robberies and murders.				
Italian workers were frustrated because they felt they were working too many hours.				
The Government in Italy did not deal effectively with the economic and social crisis in this period.				
The writer believes that the social and economic crisis in Italy had the potential to lead to the establishment of a Communist regime in Italy.				
The Communists did not come to power in Italy. Instead, a Fascist regime took the place of the Liberal State.				
Nationalist pride was an important factor in the rise of fascism in Italy.				
The economic crisis in Italy was worse in the south because economic conditions were worse in that region.				
If Italy had fallen to the Communists, other countries would have laughed and joked about it.				

SOURCE 1

From the diary of Bruno Palamenghi, a professional soldier who, despite years of service for the Liberal State, joined the Fascists in 1922.

Who can forget the state of degeneration to which the masses had been reduced in 1920–1921–1922? There were continuous strikes – the occupations of factories, plants, workshops and land were daily occurrences ... Property was not respected. The post and telegraph services worked according to the whim of the employees. The *barabba* gangs in Piedmont, the *tepa* in Lombardy, pick-pockets in Rome, *camorristi* in Naples, *Mafiosi* in Sicily, spread terror in every town, freely carrying out persecutions – abuse – brutality of every kind – robberies – murders, and other things – and all this because of the weakness of governments at the time ... Just a few months more of that regime and this beautiful Italy of ours would have been finished ... Without the Fascist revolution ... Italy would have fallen prey to communism, anarchy, bankruptcy, poverty – and we would have become the laughing-stock and joke of the other nations, worse than we were before the war.

AS-level question

How much weight do you give the evidence of Source 1 for an enquiry into the reasons why opposition to the Liberal State increased in the period 1918–22?

Explain your answer using the source, the information given about it and your own knowledge of the historical context.

Political developments, 1919

REVISED

Political reforms

After the First World War there were attempts to reform the Italian political system. In December 1918, Prime Minister Vittorio Orlando implemented **universal male suffrage** in an attempt to win more electoral support. It was meant to be a reward for soldiers who had fought in the First World War.

In 1919, Francesco Saverio Nitti introduced proportional representation, where each party was allocated a number of seats in proportion to the number of votes cast for their candidates in the Chamber of Deputies. He hoped it would weaken support for the more extreme political parties but was proven wrong.

Growth of the Socialist Party (PSI) and Catholic Party (PPI)

The adoption of universal suffrage and proportional representation led to the emergence of two mass parties: the Socialist Party (PSI) and the Catholic *Popolari* Party (PPI).

The Socialist Party (PSI)

The PSI grew to become a mass party. Italian Socialists won elections in many town councils and so controlled local taxes and services. Despite this, however, they were divided between the PSI, Socialist trade unions and Socialist councils. These groups often failed to work together effectively, and after the First World War the movement lacked a leader that could unify them. The Socialists also lacked an effective strategy to take and keep political power, despite their rising support.

In the commercialised Po Valley, Socialist agricultural unions made a range of economic demands such as higher wages and fewer working hours. They also tried to control the supply of labour and employment. They were prepared to adopt violent tactics to achieve their aims. Although all of these actions attracted supporters, it also encouraged other Italians to support more extreme political groups such as the Fascists. Mussolini skilfully exploited fears regarding socialism to gain support for the Fascists.

Popolari (PPI)

The *Popolari*, or Popular, Party was founded in January 1919 by the Sicilian priest Don Luigi Sturzo. Pope Benedict XV supported its establishment but acknowledged it would be separate from the Catholic Church. The party consisted of a coalition of Catholics who wanted to improve the living standards of Italian peasants. They supported various social reforms, including the foundations of a welfare state. They were prepared to enter coalitions with the Liberals as long as they were granted meaningful political concessions.

Result and impact of the 1919 elections

The November 1919 election result saw the PSI and the *Popolari* become the two most powerful parties in the Chamber of Deputies, with 156 and 100 Deputies respectively. Giolitti's Liberals only won 91 seats, while the right-wing Liberals won 23. The Liberals were no longer the political force they were before the First World War and they were deeply divided. Therefore, given the fact that neither the Socialists or *Popolari* had enough deputies to rule and would not work with each other, the resulting Liberal Government was weak and unstable. In 1920, Giolitti managed to establish a coalition with the *Popolari* but his anti-clerical past made his relationship with Sturzo difficult. The November 1919 elections were the beginning of the end for the Liberal State.

Simple essay style

Below are three sample exam questions. Use your own knowledge and the information in the book so far. Choose four general points, and provide three pieces of specific information to support each general point. Once you have planned each essay, write the introduction and conclusion for the essay. The introduction should list the points to be discussed in the essay. The conclusion should summarise the key points and justify which point was the most important.

How far does Italy's 'mutilated victory' after the First World War account for the weaknesses of The Liberal State in the period 1918–22?

How significant were the elections of 1919 in weakening the Liberal State in the period 1918–22?

How accurate is it to say that the Italian Liberal State was responsible for its own downfall?

Write the question

a

The following sources relate to the economic and political crisis in Italy in the period 1919–22. Read the guidance detailing what you need to know about Italy during this period. Having done this, complete an exam-style question connected with sources.

How far could the historian make use of Sources 1 and 2 together to investigate ...?

____

____

Explain your answer, using both of the sources, the information given about them and your own knowledge of the historical context.

SOURCE 1

From Angelo Tasca, a former Communist, writing in 1938 about the rise of fascism in the period 1920–22.

Out of 280 villages in Emilia 223 were in Socialist hands. The landowners were powerless before the all-powerful workers' trade unions. In the countryside the prizes of public life were almost entirely denied to the whole middle class who were not members of the Socialist organisations. The country landowner who for years had been head of the village, was ousted [from his position]. On the land he had to reckon with the [Socialist] league which controlled employment, in the market with the Socialist co-operative which fixed prices ... Profit, position, power were lost to him and his children. Hatred and bitterness were welling up, ready at any moment to overflow ... The old ruling classes felt that they were being swept away to make room for the new social structure.

SOURCE 2

From Italo Balbo, a Fascist leader in Ferrara, writing in 1932.

When I came back from the war, just like so many, I hated politics and politicians, who in my opinion had betrayed the hopes of the combatants, reducing Italy to a shameful peace and systematic humiliation of any Italians who supported the cult of heroes. Fight, combat, to come back to the country of Giolitti, who offered every ideal as an item for sale? No. Better to deny everything, to destroy everything, so as to rebuild everything from scratch. Many in those days turned to Socialism. It was the ready-made revolutionary programme and, apparently the most radical ... It is certain, in my opinion, that, without Mussolini, three-quarters of the Italian youth which had returned from the trenches would have become communists.

Mussolini and the development of fascism, 1919–22

REVISED

Foundation of the *Fasci di Combattimento* and party programme

On 23 March 1919, Benito Mussolini, a former Socialist journalist and radical, founded the new political group *Fasci di Combattimento*. The event organised to launch it was not well attended, with only 118 assorted radicals present.

The word *fascio* was increasingly being used by right-wing political groups to stand for strength and unity. Initially, Mussolini prioritised action over political theory, and the ideology of the new movement was unclear. After 1922 he tried, with the support of other Fascists, to add more depth to fascism and develop a coherent doctrine but this was never fully achieved. The *Fasci di Combattimento*'s manifesto called for:

- a minimum wage and an eight-hour working day
- the confiscation of Church property
- control of the banks and stock exchanges
- the restoration of Italy's national strength and prestige.

These policies were intended to attract support from different social classes within Italy. Every disillusioned group could find something they agreed with. Mussolini's fascism also emphasised negatives to attract political support, such as:

- the growing threat of socialism
- the weakness of the Italian political system and democracy
- the failure to maintain law and order
- the Treaty of Versailles and 'mutilated victory'.

On its way to power, the Fascist movement would dramatically change its policies.

The 1919 election

The elections of 1919 were a failure for the Fascists. They failed to win any seats in the Parliament, and achieved fewer than 5,000 votes out of 275,000 in their powerbase of Milan. It seemed that fascism was on the verge of collapse, with only 4,000 active supporters in 1919. It was Mussolini's exploitation of conservative fears of the 'Socialist threat' that saved the movement and led to its rapid growth.

Squadrismo and the move to the right

The mass worker occupation of factories in 1920 convinced many Italians they were on the verge of a revolution and that Fascists would defend Italy against this threat. Initially, fascism gained its support from urban areas and former servicemen, expanding from Milan into other northern Italian cities and towns. From early 1921 onwards, the movement of fascism from urban to rural areas resulted in more support for the Fascists. Agricultural employers called for help against local Socialist or Catholic unions, and financed the groups that were set up as a result. Fascists organised themselves into squads (squadristi), paramilitary groups often led by former army officers. They wore black shirts to identify themselves and targeted Socialists, often violently. They invaded villages, beat up union leaders, engaged in strike breaking, intimidated voters during elections and organised tax strikes in socialist-controlled towns. They were often helped by the army and the police, who saw the Fascists as a good way to regain control of certain areas.

Mussolini and the *squadristi*

Mussolini put himself forward as the leader of the Fascist movement, and took credit for the actions of the *squadristi*. Local Fascist leaders did not want to surrender their independence, however, and the radical local leaders, the *Ras*, resisted his control. Despite this, Mussolini convinced the majority of them to support him, and his newspaper *Il Popolo d'Italia* was used to publicise Fascist activities. With Mussolini as a unifying leader the movement could present itself as powerful, stable and national. In turn, Mussolini used the *squadristi* to present himself as a moderate statesmen, the only one who could keep the violence of the squads in check. In that way he tried to appeal to both the radicals and the traditional elites. By the middle of 1921, the *squadristi* controlled significant areas of the Italian countryside, placing Mussolini in a powerful position.

Support from 1921

Local leaders within rural areas, for example powerful landowners, often supported the *squadristi*. The Fascist movement now appealed to shopkeepers and wealthier farmers. Small-scale industrialists angry at the tax increases and economic problems also played a role in supporting and financing local Fascist groups.

Younger Italians saw fascism as an appealing alternative to the corrupt Liberal system while older generations saw it as promoting stability. At the same time, fascism still appealed to radicals like **Italo Balbo** or **Roberto Farinacci**, who believed in the violent overthrow of the state by force.

Add the context

Below is a sample exam question with the accompanying sources. Having read the question and the sources, complete the following activity.

How far could the historian make use of Sources 1 and 2 together to investigate Fascist violence in the years 1919–22?

First, look for aspects of the source that refer to the events and discussion that were going on around the time that the source was written. Underline the key phrases and write a brief description of the context in the margin next to the source. Draw an arrow from the key phrase to the context. Try to find three key phrases in each source.

SOURCE 1

From a telegram sent by a local Deputy, Luigi Fabbri, to Bonomi, the Prime Minister and Minister of the Interior, on 1 October 1921.

Must report to your Excellency the very grave situation which has been created in the town of Budrio. Terrorised by an unpunished Fascist band using clubs, revolvers, etc. Union organisers and municipal administrators forced to leave for fear of death. Workers forced to lock themselves at home because of continuous beatings and threats of beatings. Unions and socialist club ordered to dissolve themselves within 48 hours or face physical destruction. Life of town is paralysed, authorities impotent. Mass of the workers request energetic measures to protect their freedom of association and personal safety.

SOURCE 2

From the diary of Italo Balbo, a senior Fascist, from Ravenna in early 1922.

We had to strike terror into the heart of our enemies. I announced to [the police chief] that I would burn down and destroy the houses of Socialists in Ravenna if he did not give me within half an hour the means required for sending the Fascists elsewhere. I demanded a whole fleet of lorries. The police officers ... told me where I could find lorries already supplied with petrol. Some of them actually belonged to the office of the police chief ... We went through all the towns and centres in the provinces of Forli and Ravenna and destroyed and burnt all the red buildings, the seats of the Socialist and Communist organisations ... The whole plain of the Romagna was given up to the reprisals of the outraged Fascists determined to break for ever the red terror.

Use the context

a

Having completed the previous activity, read the following statements and work out how to use the context to support the following claims.

Write a sentence justifying each of the claims in the space provided:

Source 1 is correct to suggest that the 'mass of the workers' did not support Fascist violence because ...

Source 2's description of the influence of the Socialist Party as 'the red terror' reflects the writer's political position because ...

The fact that Source 1 and Source 2 provide similar accounts of the nature of Fascist violence in this period makes them more valuable to a historian because ...

Political legitimacy, the PNF, the 'New Programme' and the nature and extent of Fascist support in 1922

REVISED

Mussolini's policy of trying to appeal to both his radical urban followers and establishment figures has been referred to as a 'dual policy'. Fascism was clearly moving away from its left-wing roots to a much more conservative or right-wing stance. Some radical policies were dropped, for example republicanism and anti-clericalism. Fascism was changing rapidly.

In July 1921, Mussolini proposed a 'pact of pacification' between the Fascists and the Socialist trade unions. Conservative supporters did not want the violence of the *squadristi* to go too far, and the 'pact of pacification' made Mussolini look like a peacemaker. The pact itself failed, as many Fascist leaders rejected it and looked about for a new leader. It threatened to split the movement but no clear alternative to Mussolini existed, so he survived in position when he abandoned the pact. Mussolini sought other ways to achieve political legitimacy.

The foundation of the National Fascist Party (PNF), October 1921

Mussolini announced the creation of a formal Fascist political party known as the *Partito Nazionale Fascista* (PNF) in October 1921. It provided more co-ordination to the movement and gave Mussolini greater control. Local branches were set up, 'respectable' recruits attracted and membership dues collected, in contrast to the looser organisation of the violent squads. Those in control of the party were from Mussolini's Milan powerbase and were loyal to him. From this point he was also able to take part in political negotiations legitimately with other parties. Membership grew quickly, from 200,000 members in 1921 to 300,000 by 1922, and it became the party of the respectable middle classes of Italy. As such, other political parties began considering including the Fascists in coalitions and in government, in order to 'normalise' them and make them less radical.

The 'New Programme'

The main appeal of the Fascists was their anti-socialism, their emphasis on patriotism and the leadership cult of Mussolini. In November 1921, the Fascist political programme included the following points, among others:

- an eight-hour working day with exceptions for agricultural or industrial needs
- limiting citizen freedoms in relation to the needs of the nation
- taxes should be proportional to income and there should be no forcible confiscations
- there were no references to confiscating the property of the Catholic Church
- military service should be obligatory
- Italy's influence in the Mediterranean should be expanded.

In November 1921, Mussolini declared his opposition to divorce, in an attempt to attract the support of Catholics. He knew he needed to remove or weaken earlier radical Fascist demands for economic and social reform to make fascism more appealing to conservatives. From 1921, Mussolini emphasised what he opposed instead of what he supported, giving vague speeches that lacked detailed outlines of his policies. He benefited further from the weakness of the other political parties, such as the *Popolari*, which was not supported by the Pope after 1922.

The nature and extent of Fascist support in 1922

By 1922, support for the Fascist movement and for Mussolini personally had increased dramatically. He continued to exploit middle- and upper-class fears of a Socialist revolution, and moved fascism increasingly to the right. In 1922, the key support for fascism came from:

- landowners and civil servants
- shopkeepers, small merchants and small business owners
- teachers and university students
- artisans and skilled craftsmen.

These supporters were drawn from a wide range of backgrounds but all of them felt insecure about their economic future and were worried about the threat of socialism towards their jobs, land and social class. Fascism had the advantage of being a movement that appealed to students while also appealing to their more conservative parents. In rural areas, fascism appealed to wealthier peasants or small-scale landowners who felt threatened by Socialist policies regarding land redistribution and tax. The Socialist Land Leagues, which intimidated farmers into hiring workers when they were not needed, also drew landowners to the Fascists, who they saw as bringing the return of law and order.

Fascist syndicates

As the Fascists gained greater control in the early 1920s and broke up Socialist and Catholic trade unions, workers were forced to join Fascist syndicates to gain employment. Some were attracted to the Fascists because they disliked the violence used by Socialist trade unions against those who refused to co-operate with strikers, while others were driven by the necessity of gaining work. Other workers liked Fascist policies on fair wages and prices, or providing peasants with land. Employers tolerated this because it was viewed as a good alternative to socialism.

Qualify your judgement

Below is a sample exam question with the accompanying sources. Having read the question and the sources, complete the following activity.

How far could the historian make use of Sources 1 and 2 together to investigate the appeal of fascism in Italy in the period 1920–22?

Below are three judgements about the value of Source 1 to a historian investigating the appeal of fascism in Italy in the period 1920–22. Circle the judgement that best describes the value of the source, and explain why it is the best in the space provided.

1. Source 1 is valuable to a historian investigating the appeal of fascism in Italy in the period 1920–22 because it provides evidence of the promises made by Mussolini in an attempt to win the support of the Italian population.
2. Source 1 is unreliable to a historian because it is by Mussolini and so it is biased.
3. Source 1 is partially valuable to a historian investigating the appeal of fascism in Italy in the period 1920–22 because it provides evidence of the promises made by Mussolini in an attempt to win the support of the Italian population. However, it is less useful for revealing the extent of support for fascism at this time, as it does not describe how people reacted to Mussolini's speech.

The best judgement about the value of Source 1 is:

____

because...

____

Now apply what you have learnt by writing a judgement about the value of Source 2 for a historian investigating the appeal of fascism in Italy in the period 1920–22.

____

____

SOURCE 1

From a speech by Mussolini in the city of Udine in September 1922.

Our programme is simple: we wish to govern Italy. We must have a State which will simply say: 'The State does not represent a party, it represents the nation as a whole, it includes all, is over all, protects all.' A State ... which is not like the Liberal State ... a State which does not fall under the power of the Socialists ... We [also] want to remove from the State all its economic attributes. We have had enough of the State railwayman, the State postman and the State insurance official. We have had enough of the State administration at the expense of Italian taxpayers, which has done nothing but aggravate the exhausted financial condition of the country. [The new state will] still control the police, who protect honest men from the attacks of thieves ... [and] the army that must guarantee the inviolability of the country and foreign policy.

SOURCE 2

From You Can't Print That!, *by the American journalist George Seldes, published in 1929. He is describing a speech given by Mussolini in the early 1920s.*

He began coldly, in a voice northern and unimpassioned. I had never heard an Italian orator so restrained. Then he changed, became soft and warm, added gestures, and flames in his eyes. The audience moved with him. He held them. Suddenly he lowered his voice to a heavy whisper and the silence among the listeners became more intense. The whisper sank lower and the listeners strained breathlessly to hear. Then Mussolini exploded with thunder and fire, and the mob – for it was no more than a mob now – rose to its feet and shouted. Immediately Mussolini became cold and restrained again and swept his mob into its seats exhausted. An actor. Actor extraordinary, with a country for a stage, a great powerful histrionic ego, swaying an audience of millions, confounding the world by his theatrical cleverness.

Mussolini gains power, 1920–22

REVISED

Political unrest

In June 1920, Nitti's Government collapsed and Giolitti established a new coalition. This Government was also unstable, however, and the May 1921 elections resulted in the Fascists gaining seats in the Chamber of Deputies. Alongside the establishment of the PNF, this gave Mussolini an element of respectability, and enabled him to withdraw his support from Giolitti. He argued only he could save Italy from socialism.

Governmental instability

The post-war governments seemed unable to deal with the economic and social consequences of the First World War, and were seen as weak as a consequence. Furthermore, parties that could have united against the Fascists failed to work together. Between 1919 and 1922, five successive governments collapsed, leading to further uncertainty.

In 1921, before the elections, Giolitti included the Fascists in the government bloc electoral list in order to try to bring them within the Liberal State. This was a big mistake, giving the Fascists an air of legitimacy and a foothold in government. It weakened official resistance to Fascist violence. In December 1921, Giolitti's successor, Bonomi, tried to control the squads, but action was not taken in most places. Alongside an awareness of the popularity of fascism, this meant that Fascist violence was virtually tolerated.

The general strike, July 1922

On 31 July 1922, the Socialists called a general strike. This gave the Fascists an excuse to attack strikers openly in cities across the country. Although the strike collapsed due to lack of support after only a day, Fascists fought running battles with Socialists across the country. The Fascists burned down the building that housed the Socialist newspaper *Avanti!* They also took over the running of the trains to break the transport workers' strike. The Fascists took the credit for ending the strike, promoting the view that the government was weak and that the Fascists were the only ones taking the initiative against socialism. Italian elites became increasingly convinced that Mussolini needed to be brought into a coalition government to help deal with the threat of socialism.

Establishing a dual policy

By October 1922, Mussolini had developed a dual policy to gain power:

- encouraging **blackshirt** violence, drawing up plans for a blackshirt seizure of power
- working with established politicians to persuade them that the PNF was a serious political movement that could work in coalition.

This looks contradictory but Mussolini used the two elements to reinforce each other. Giolitti was forced to listen because Mussolini had the backing of the blackshirts, and could use force. But Mussolini also knew that the blackshirts were no match for the Italian army. Both aspects strengthened his negotiating position.

Support your judgement

Below are a sample exam question and two basic judgements. Read the exam question and the two judgements. Support the judgement that you agree with most strongly by adding a reason that justifies the judgement.

> 'Support for fascism in the early 1920s was due to dissatisfaction with the Liberal State rather than the appeal of Fascist actions and policies.' How far do you agree with this statement?

Tip: whichever option you choose you will have to weigh up both sides of the argument.

Overall, the main reason why fascism gained support in the early 1920s was dissatisfaction with the Liberal State.

Overall, the main reason why fascism gained support in the early 1920s was the appeal of Fascist actions and policies.

Select the detail

Below is a sample AS exam question with the accompanying source. Having read the question and the source, complete the following activity

> Why is Source 1 valuable to the historian for an enquiry into the causes of Fascist violence in Italy in the period 1920–22?

Below are three claims that you could make when answering the question. Read the claims and then select quotes from the sources to support them.

Source 1 is valuable to the historian for an enquiry into the causes of Fascist violence in Italy in the period 1920–22 because it explains that the Fascists used violence to attack their political enemies.

Source 1 is valuable to the historian for an enquiry into the causes of Fascist violence in Italy in the period 1920–22 because it suggests that the Fascists believed they were using violence only in retaliation.

Source 1 is valuable to the historian for an enquiry into the causes of Fascist violence in Italy in the period 1920–22 because it suggests that the Fascists should use violence only as a last resort.

SOURCE 1

From a speech by Mussolini to Fascists in Bologna in April 1922.

We Fascists have a clear programme: we must move on led by a pillar of fire, because we are slandered and not understood. And, however much violence may be deplored, it is evident that we, in order to make our ideas understood, must beat refractory [obstinate] skulls with resounding blows ... But we do not make a school, a system or, worse still, an aesthetic [thing of beauty] of violence. We are violent because it is necessary to be so.

Our punitive expeditions, all those acts of violence which feature in the papers, must always have the character of ... legitimate reprisal: because we are the first to recognise that it is sad, after having fought the external enemy, to have to fight the enemy within ... The Socialists had formed a state within a state ... [and] this state is more tyrannical, illiberal and overbearing than the old one; and for this reason what we are causing today is a revolution to break up the Bolshevik state, while waiting to settle our accounts with the Liberal State which remains.

The March on Rome and its significance

REVISED

The March on Rome, October 1922

This was to be the next step in establishing Fascist domination over Italian politics. On 16 October Mussolini and other Fascist leaders made plans for a march on Rome to take place on 28 October. It was deliberately meant to mimic the Italian hero Garibaldi's march on Rome in the 1860s during the process of unification. Fascists were meant to descend on Rome from across Italy.

Mussolini was more doubtful than other Fascist leaders because he thought it might lose them their air of respectability, while radicals wanted a violent seizure of power. Mussolini hoped the march would persuade the authorities to give him power anyway.

On 27 October the *squadristi* gathered at three locations around 20 miles from Rome. They also tried to seize government buildings in towns around northern and central Italy. It added to the atmosphere of intimidation. In reality, the turnout for the march was not good, and the *squadristi* were poorly armed.

Despite this, it was a propaganda coup, and the threat succeeded as Mussolini hoped it would. Prime Minister Facta's Government resigned, although he was asked to stay on. He tried to resist but his ability to do so rested on the King, Victor Emmanuel III.

The role of Victor Emmanuel III

King Victor Emmanuel III played a vital role in enabling Mussolini to take power. He made two key decisions:

- He eventually refused to authorise the use of martial law against the March of Rome, after initially agreeing to it.
- He supported the appointment of Mussolini as Prime Minister on 30 October 1922, after initially hoping Mussolini would serve in a government headed by Antonio Salandra. Mussolini refused to accept anything but the premiership.

The King supported Mussolini for several reasons.

- He was afraid of the potential for civil war and was unsure the army was strong enough to crush the Fascists and the Socialists. He was unconvinced the army would follow orders to attack the Fascists as they had a lot of support in the military.
- The King's cousin, the Duke of Aosta, was a Fascist supporter who wanted to topple the King and take the throne. The King was aware of the threat and did not want to give Aosta an excuse to remove him if he acted against the Fascists.
- He hoped to be able to exert more control over Mussolini if he was part of the government.
- The traditional political system was collapsing and could not provide political stability. There seemed to be no alternative but to invite Mussolini to be the next Prime Minister of Italy.

Mussolini's appointment as Prime Minister

Mussolini was appointed Prime Minister on 30 October 1922. He took the overnight train from the Swiss border and arrived in Rome at 10.42 am. He wore his black shirt and was formally asked to form the next government. He was sworn in as Prime Minister the next day, becoming Italy's youngest ever Prime Minister at only 39 years old.

After 1922, the March on Rome was depicted as the catalyst for Mussolini taking power, but the events did not match the propaganda. Mussolini arrived in Rome before the Fascist supporters even arrived, and there was no violent takeover of power. The 50,000 blackshirts and army troops that marched through Rome on 31 October were celebrating the achievement of political power.

Spectrum of importance

Below is a sample exam question and a list of general points which could be used to answer the question. Use your own knowledge and the information on the opposite page to reach a judgement about the importance of these general points to the question posed. Write numbers on the spectrum below to indicate their relative importance. Having done this, write a brief justification of your placement, explaining why some of these factors are more important than others. The resulting diagram could form the basis of an essay plan.

How far was the impact of the First World War the main reason why Mussolini was appointed Prime Minister in October 1922?

1 The impact of the First World War

2 Political divisions

3 Fear of socialism

4 The impact of the invasion of Fiume

5 The organisation and policies of Italian Fascists

6 The actions of the King

Less important ⟷ Very important

Introducing an argument

Below are a sample exam question, a list of key points to be made in the essay and a simple introduction and conclusion for the essay. Read the question, the plan and the introduction and conclusion. Rewrite the introduction and the conclusion in order to develop an argument.

How far was the impact of the First World War the main reason why Mussolini was appointed Prime Minister in October 1922?

Key points

- The impact of the First World War
- Political divisions
- Fear of socialism
- The impact of the invasion of Fiume
- The organisation and policies of Italian Fascists
- The actions of the King

Introduction

There were six key reasons why Mussolini was appointed Prime Minister in October 1922. The most important reason was the impact of the First World War. These included the impact of the First World War, political divisions, a fear of socialism and the impact of the invasion of Fiume. In addition, the organisation and policies of Italian Fascists and the actions of the King also played a role.

Conclusion

In conclusion, there were six key reasons why Mussolini was appointed Prime Minister in October 1922. The most important reason was the impact of the First World War. This played a more significant role than all of the other factors.

The creation of a Fascist dictatorship, 1922–26

REVISED

Parliamentary compromise and coercion

Mussolini was still in a vulnerable position in October 1922, and relied on parliamentary support, but by 1925 he dominated the Italian political system. His first steps towards achieving such control were very important. Initially the majority of Deputies in his government were not Fascist party members. Only 32 out of the 535 Deputies were from the PNF. He headed a largely right-wing coalition. In his 'National Government' only four were Fascists, alongside four Liberals, two *Popolari* Deputies, one Nationalist and three independents.

The Chamber of Deputies met on 16 November 1922. Mussolini delivered a controversial speech, indicating the Fascists were prepared to close the parliament and demanding full powers that would allow him to govern by himself. He promised to uphold constitutional liberties but made it clear he could dissolve the Chamber whenever he saw fit. With these promises and threats, Italian Deputies voted to grant Mussolini the powers he wanted for one year.

Mussolini used a mixture of political intimidation and compromise with his key political rivals. He needed control over the existing state institutions in order to maintain his dominance over the more radical Fascists, especially the *Ras* in the provinces.

Controlling the PNF

After becoming Prime Minister, Mussolini tried to exert more control over the PNF and the *squadristi*. Mussolini wanted to end the violence of the *Ras* and the *squadristi* and return to normal constitutional political methods. To do this he made concessions to the Catholic Church and passed measures favourable to industrialists and landowners. The radical Roberto Farinacci was made party secretary by Mussolini, which gave him more control over the radical branch of the party. Mussolini sent another radical, Cesare de Vecchi, to govern Italian Somaliland in order to prevent his continued violent action against local opposition. Mussolini wanted to avoid a political reaction against the Fascist movement at this time.

The Fascist militia

Mussolini knew that he needed to keep the support of the Fascist *squadristi* since they had performed a vital role in his rise to power, but he also needed to keep them under control. To do this he created the Fascist Militia (MSVN) in January 1923 to 'defend the Fascist revolution'. The MSVN consisted of 300,000 blackshirts who were paid directly by the state. Mussolini was head of the organisation so could control them more easily than before. The authority of the *Ras* was weakened by new commanders, and more than 200 *Ras* were expelled from the party.

The MSVN provided employment to Fascists around Italy, who were given uniforms and encouraged to keep a high profile. Actually they had no real political power, but served mainly to strengthen Mussolini's control over the Fascist movement.

The Fascist Grand Council, December 1922

In December 1922 Mussolini created the **Grand Council of Fascism** to reassure leading Fascists of their significance. It was to act as a consultative committee where Fascist leaders would meet to discuss political issues. It also linked the broader Fascist movement and the Fascist Government. This had two purposes for Mussolini:

- He could exert his control over leading members of the Fascist movement.
- The Grand Council was designed to discuss policy before it was sent to the cabinet and parliament for approval. This meant new policy was created by the Fascist party, not the elected parliament.

Mussolini chose the 22 members of the Council, which met once a month.

Growth in PNF membership

PNF membership grew from 300,000 in October 1922 to 783,000 by the end of 1923. This helped to dilute the more radical elements of the Fascist movement who might have opposed Mussolini's policy of normalisation. New members weren't necessarily believers, but wanted the patronage the PNF could offer. The Italian Nationalists merged with the PNF in February 1923, which brought more conservative and upper-class members to the PNF.

Select the detail

Below is a sample A-level exam question with the accompanying sources. Having read the question and the sources, complete the following activity.

How far could the historian make use of Sources 1 and 2 together to investigate the ways in which Mussolini dealt with his political rivals in the period 1920–23?

Below are three claims that you could make when answering the question. Read the claims and then select quotes from the sources to support them. Copy down the quotes in the space provided.

Tip: keep the quotes short, never copy more than a sentence. Remember, sometimes a few words embedded in a sentence is all you need to support your claims.

Source 1 is useful because it shows how Mussolini attempted to appease other political parties.

Source 2 is useful because it shows how Mussolini attempted to deal with Fascist radicals.

Both sources are useful because they contain evidence about the way in which Mussolini used threats to remove opposition to his Government.

SOURCE 1

From a speech given by Mussolini in parliament on 16 November 1922.

The increase of a nation's prestige in the world is proportionate to the discipline that the country displays at home. There is no doubt that the domestic situation has improved, but not as much as I should like ... Acts of violence are sporadic and peripheral, but they must come to an end. All citizens, regardless of party, must be able to move about freely.

All religious beliefs must be respected, with particular consideration for the dominant one, Catholicism. Fundamental freedoms must not be impaired; respect for the law must be exacted at whatever cost. The state is strong, and it intends to show its strength against everyone, even against any eventual Fascist illegality, for this would be an irresponsible and impure illegality wholly lacking in justification. I must add, however, that nearly all Fascists have given complete support to the new order of things ... The state does not intend to abdicate its authority before anyone. Whoever defies the state will be punished. This explicit warning is addressed to all citizens ... The state will undertake to prune and perfect the armed forces that guard it.

We ask for full powers because we wish to assume full responsibility. We propose to give discipline to the nation.

SOURCE 2

From Royal Decree No. 31, 14 January 1923. This decree created the Fascist Militia.

The Voluntary Militia for National Security is hereby established.

The Militia for National Security will serve God and the Italian fatherland, and will be under the orders of the Head of the Government. With the help of the Armed Corps of Public Security and the Royal Army, it will be responsible for maintaining public order within the nation; and it will train and organise citizens for the defence of Italy's interests in the world.

All parties whatsoever shall be forbidden to have formations of a military character after the present decree goes into effect. Violators will be subject to punishment by law.

The present decree will be presented to Parliament for enactment into law and will go into force on 1 February 1923.

The Acerbo Law and Matteotti Crisis, 1923–24

REVISED

The Acerbo Law, 1923

The **Acerbo Law** was proposed by the Fascist Giacomo Acerbo and drafted by the Fascist Grand Council, and dramatically changed the electoral system of Italy. It was passed in July 1923 by the Chamber of Deputies and came into effect in the April 1924 elections. In the Acerbo Law Mussolini sought to end the system of proportional representation and give himself more control over Italian politics and power. The proposals were as follows:

- Elections would be organised in the same way, with political parties producing lists of constituency candidates.
- Votes cast would be totalled and the party list which gained the most votes would then be allocated two-thirds of the seats within the Chamber of Deputies, as long as they had at least 25 per cent of the votes cast.
- The remaining one-third of the seats would be allocated to the other lists in proportion to the votes they had gained.

The Acerbo Law gained support from Liberals as well as Fascists because they thought it would end the ongoing political instability in Italy. Right-wing Liberals also thought it would undermine support for the Socialists as they often struggled to build links to other parties or groups. Mussolini knew, however, that many local councils were dominated by Fascists and Fascist squads could be used to intimidate voters and fix elections, leading to a permanent Fascist majority in parliament.

Mussolini threatened to close the Chamber of Deputies if the Acerbo Law was not passed, and arranged for armed blackshirts to be present in the Chamber to intimidate politicians during the discussions. Mussolini's decision to pass laws favourable to the Catholic Church meant that the Pope pressurised the *Popolari* to support the proposals. In the end, only the Socialists and Communists opposed the Acerbo Law.

The 1924 elections

Elections were held in April 1924, and the Fascists joined forces with right-wing Liberals such as Salandra during the campaign. The Fascists and their allies gained 66 per cent of the vote and the number of Fascist MPs increased from 35 to 374. This meant Mussolini had a clear majority within the Chamber of Deputies, achieved via a mixture of genuine popularity, violence, intimidation and ballot rigging. Mussolini did not have total power, however, as laws still had to be approved by parliament, there were still opposition groups and the King still had the power to dismiss him.

The Matteotti Crisis, 1924

On 30 May 1924, a leading Socialist, **Giacomo Matteotti**, presented evidence to parliament about Fascist violence and the influence of terror on the outcome of the April 1924 elections. He called for the annulment of the election results and for fresh elections. Only 11 days afterwards Matteotti was kidnapped by Fascists and stabbed to death. This created a political storm, shocked world opinion and caused widespread criticism of Mussolini and the Fascists.

Mussolini denied having prior knowledge of the assassination, but evidence began to emerge that linked him with the murder. Many believed the *Ceka*, a secret hit squad set up by Mussolini, were directly involved. Several prominent Fascists were arrested, and some opposition MPs withdrew from the Chamber of Deputies and established a rival parliament. They hoped to persuade the King to dismiss Mussolini, but the King refused, fearing an increase in Socialist influence.

Mussolini survived the Matteotti crisis and made further moves to secure his position in the summer of 1924:

- Press censorship was introduced in July 1924.
- All meetings by opposition groups or parties were banned in August 1924.

Fascist pressure on Mussolini

In December 1924, 33 leading Fascists approached Mussolini and demanded he establish a dictatorship. They threatened to withdraw their support if he did not agree to their demands, and so on 3 January 1925 Mussolini announced to the Italian parliament than he would set up a dictatorship within 48 hours.

Establish criteria

Below is a sample exam question which requires you to make a judgement. The key term in the question has been underlined. Defining the meaning of the key term can help you establish criteria that you can use to make a judgement.

Read the question, define the key term and then set out two or three criteria based on the key term which you can use to reach and justify a judgement.

> How accurate is it to say that Mussolini <u>successfully consolidated</u> Fascist power over Italy in the period 1922–25?

Definition:

____

____

Criteria to judge the extent to which Mussolini successfully consolidated Fascist power over Italy in the period 1922–25:

- ______________________________
- ______________________________
- ______________________________

Reach a judgement

Having defined the key term and established a series of criteria, you should now make a judgement. Consider how successfully Mussolini consolidated Fascist power over Italy in the period 1922–25 according to each criterion. Summarise your judgements below:

Criterion 1:

____

Criterion 2:

____

Criterion 3:

____

Criterion 4:

____

Finally, sum up your judgement. Based on the criteria, how accurate is it to say that Mussolini successfully consolidated Fascist power over Italy in the period 1922–25?

____

____

____

Tip: remember you should weigh up evidence of successful consolidation against evidence of limited consolidation in your conclusion.

Repression in 1925 and constitutional amendments, 1925–26

REVISED

Throughout 1925, Mussolini took steps to dismantle potential opposition to his rule.

The press

Mussolini tightened press censorship and newspaper owners were pressured to dismiss editors who had been critical of the Fascists. After December 1925, all journalists had to have their names on an official register (controlled by the Fascists) before they could seek employment. It gave the Fascists great control over news stories in Italy.

Ban on political parties

In 1925, the Pope withdrew support for the *Popolari,* which disintegrated. The Deputies who walked out of parliament after Matteotti's murder were not allowed to return, and in December 1925 Mussolini passed a law that strengthened the power of central government. This banned all political opposition groups and non-Fascist trade unions. Freedom of association – the freedom to meet together, particularly in political groups – was ended on 25 November 1926, although it had been greatly restricted since 1922.

The police

The powers of the police forces were strengthened, enabling them to take action against real or suspected opponents of the regime.

Constitutional amendments

The constitution of the Liberal State was destroyed in 1925–26.

The *Legge Fascistissime*, December 1925

- All opposition parties were formally banned.
- Locally elected mayors and councils were replaced by officials appointed by the Government.
- A new secret police, the **OVRA**, was established, and additional courts were set up to try political offences.
- A new post of Head of Government was created for Mussolini. Henceforth he would be known as *Il Duce* (the leader) rather than Prime Minister. Mussolini was no longer responsible to parliament, and could only be dismissed by the King.

The *Legge Fascistissime* transformed Mussolini's Government into a legal dictatorship.

Rule by decree, 1926

In January 1926, Mussolini was given the power to rule by decree. In that month alone some 20,000 decrees were issued.

Complete the table

Mussolini faced a number of obstacles in his plan to establish a Fascist dictatorship in Italy. Use the information on the opposite page and the previous two spreads to complete the table below, explaining how he removed these obstacles to his power.

Obstacle	Ways in which Mussolini removed this obstacle
The Italian political system	
Other political parties	
Radicals within the Fascist movement	
The press	
The legal system	
The Catholic Church	

Identify the concept

Below are five sample exam questions based on some of the following concepts:

- Cause questions concern the reasons for something, or why something happened.
- Consequence questions concern the impact of an event, an action or a policy.
- Change/continuity questions ask you to investigate the extent to which things changed or stayed the same.
- Similarity/difference questions ask you to investigate the extent to which two events, actions or policies were similar.
- Significance questions concern the importance of an event, an action or a policy.

Read each of the questions and work out which of the concepts they are based on.

How far were the elections of 1919 the most important turning point in the collapse of the Liberal State in Italy?

How far do you agree that the consolidation of Fascist power in the years 1922–26 was mainly due to the use of terror and violence?

'The Fascist movement in 1926 was unrecognisable from its beginnings in 1919.' How far do you agree with this statement?

How accurate is it to say that the Italian Liberal State was responsible for its own downfall?

How far did Mussolini transform the Italian political system in the years 1922–26?

Recommended reading

- A. Lyttelton (ed.), *Liberal and Fascist Italy* (Oxford University Press, 2002). Chapters 2 and 3.
- C. Duggan, *Fascist Voices: An Intimate History of Mussolini's Italy* (The Bodley Head, 2012). Chapters 3 and 4.
- J. Pollard, *The Fascist Experience in Italy* (Routledge, 1998). Chapter 2.

Exam focus

REVISED

Below is an exam-style question and a high-level answer. Read it and the comments around it.

How far does Italy's 'mutilated victory' explain growing support for the Italian Fascist Party in the years 1919–22?

Italy's 'mutilated victory' was clearly one reason for the growing support for the Italian Fascist Party in the years immediately following the First World War. However, the most important reason was the war itself. Other factors included the radical example of D'Annunzio and the appeal of fascism.

The introduction indicates that the essay will discuss four major factors. It asserts that the First World War was the most important factor, but it does not support this with an argument or with evidence.

Italy's 'mutilated victory' certainly led to growing support for the Italian Fascist Party. At the end of the First World War Italy failed to gain the territory that many Nationalists thought it deserved. Having won the war, Italy demanded new territory including the port of Fiume, South Tyrol, Trentino, Istria, parts of Dalmatia and overseas colonies that had once belonged to Turkey. However, except for South Tyrol, Trentino and Istria, the Italian Government failed to gain these territories in negotiations over the 1919 Treaty of Saint-Germain. This failure, which the radical Nationalist poet D'Annunzio called the 'mutilated victory', led many Italians to believe that the Liberal State and traditional politicians had failed Italy. The 'mutilated victory' led to growing support for the Italian Fascist Party because many radical Nationalists felt that, unlike traditional politicians, the Fascists would always put Italy first.

The first sentence of the paragraph contains a clear link to the question, suggesting that the paragraph will be focused on the question.

However, the First World War was the main reason for the growth in support for the Fascist Party in 1919–22. The First World War had many consequences for Italian politics. First, during the war Italian democracy was eroded. The war led to a growth in the power of the Prime Minister and a reduction in the power of Parliament. Also it led to the growth in power of unelected military leaders. Fascists would later argue that the success of Italy's war effort proved that these undemocratic methods were more effective than democratic methods. Also, the war led to discontent. Workers and peasants were angry that they worked hard to support the war effort, but big business profited. Indeed, workers had to work a 75-hour week. Soldiers were also angry at profiteers who had made money while they fought. Soldiers also objected to the workers who went on strike during the war. The war led to a growth in support for the Fascists because they represented a group who were prepared to continue using undemocratic methods and a group who wanted the whole nation to sacrifice the common good rather than allowing some groups to shirk their responsibilities or make profit at the expense of the nation.

The last sentence of the paragraph clearly explains how changes brought about by the First World War led to growing support for fascism.

D'Annunzio's occupation of Fiume also led to the rise of fascism. To many Nationalists, D'Annunzio seemed to be a new type of politician. D'Annunzio became a national hero during the First World War for his heroics as a soldier. In September 1919 he led around 2,000 Italian soldiers into Fiume and took by force what Italian politicians had failed to gain by negotiation. While in power in Fiume, D'Annunzio organised a new radical kind of Nationalist politics which made use of theatrical ceremonies and parades. For many Nationalists this was an attractive alternative to traditional Italian politics. Whereas traditional politicians had failed Italy in their negotiations, D'Annunzio used force to take what he felt Italy deserved. D'Annunzio's actions in Fiume helped increase support for fascism because the Fascists seemed to offer Italy an effective, heroic and radical alternative to traditional politics, just like D'Annunzio had offered Fiume.

This paragraph effectively contrasts the apparent failure of traditional politics with the apparent success of D'Annunzio's radical alternative. It concludes by linking this to fascism.

As well as the failings of traditional politics, fascism was also attractive to many Italians. Many Nationalists respected Fasci di Combattimento. These groups were made up of heroic ex-soldiers who had fought bravely for Italy. Unlike traditional politicians they had achieved a true victory rather than letting Italy down through failed negotiations. Also, the squadristi were attractive because they functioned more like an army than like a traditional political party. Again, this appealed to many who felt the army had succeeded where traditional politics had failed. Also the squadristi fought an effective 'guerrilla war' against socialism, again standing up to Socialists in a way that traditional politicians like Giolitti had failed to. Finally, Mussolini's promises to subordinate individual freedoms to the national interest as part of his radical Nationalist 'New Programme' of 1921 persuaded many Nationalists that the Fascists were a dynamic new force who could lead the nation where traditional leaders had failed.

This paragraph uses technical terms such as squadristi and specific dates to increase the level of detail used in the essay.

In conclusion, Italy's 'mutilated victory' was only one reason for the growing support for the Italian Fascist party. However, other factors included the impact of the First World War and the radicalism of D'Annunzio, the squadristi and Mussolini's 1921 'New Programme' also played a part in the growth of support for the Italian Fascist party in the years 1919–22.

This paragraph summarises the rest of the essay, but does not give an overall argument.

This is a well-focused essay which includes a large amount of relevant detail. Every paragraph presents a coherent analysis of the factor it discusses. Nonetheless, this essay cannot enter Level 5 because the introduction and conclusion simply summarise the essay and there is no attempt to develop an overall argument. Indeed, while the essay asserts that the war was the most important factor, it does not put forward an argument to prove this.

Exam focus activity

This essay achieves a Level 4. Refer to the mark scheme on page 99 as well as the comments around this essay and make a list of the features required to push a Level 4 essay into Level 5.

AS-level questions

How accurate is it to say that Mussolini came to power through popular support?

How far were the post-war economic problems a factor in the rise of fascism in the years 1919–26?

3 The Fascist State, 1925–40

Consent and control

REVISED

After Mussolini and the Fascists had achieved control and dominated Italian politics they looked for new ways to strengthen their control over the Italian population. They did this by using a mixture of consent and control.

Indoctrination of education and youth

The Fascist regime believed it was important to indoctrinate young people so they would support the new state. It created new organisations to do this and changed the curriculum. Although not all young people became Fascists as a result, it did have some success.

Fascism and schools

Fascist education policies from 1929 focused on obedience and indoctrination rather than improving standards. From the late 1920s these policies were introduced:

- A portrait of Mussolini was to be hung up in every classroom. Teachers had to refer to his genius and heroic qualities.
- Wall posters emphasised Fascist achievements.
- Every school day began with Fascist slogans.
- Primary school children were taught to read by using books with Fascist cartoons and quotations by Mussolini. Children were taught unquestioning obedience.
- From 1928 there was only one authorised textbook, focusing on Italian achievements in history and literature.
- There was an increased emphasis on sport and exercise, as well as on religious instruction.

Teachers who did not agree with these changes were dismissed, and from 1931 those who remained had to take a loyalty oath to the regime. In 1933, all teachers were required to be members of the PNF.

Fascism in the universities

The Government believed that university students would have been indoctrinated while at school, so they were less of a priority. Students were still expected to join the *Gioventi Universitaria Fascista*, or University Fascist Youth. There were some advantages to joining – students could benefit from:

- use of sports facilities
- half-price admission to entertainment
- partial exemption from military service
- enhanced career prospects.

The number of university students increased greatly and came from a diverse range of backgrounds. University students were seen as the future of the Fascist movement.

The university staff were the biggest problem for the Fascists. Professors and lecturers were harder to dismiss than teachers and more resistant to threats. Some took the loyalty oaths and joined the PNF as a 'formality', and a few refused. Some, however, were convinced Fascists.

Fascist youth movements

In 1926, youth organisations were set up for children and teenagers outside of school, under the umbrella organisation *Opera Nazionale Balilla*, known as the ONB or *Balilla*.

The children were exposed to Fascist propaganda but also took part in a wide range of activities. Girls were given more traditionally feminine activities so they could be good Fascist wives in the future. The organisations offered free sports facilities, holidays at the seaside for urban children and scholarships for the gifted.

Members had to swear a loyalty oath, learn a special *Balilla* creed and wear a uniform. These organisations were not popular with all children and faced opposition from rival organisations run by the Catholic Church. The Church's movement was eventually banned, after which membership rapidly rose, only to collapse completely as soon as Mussolini was removed from power.

Opera Nazionale Dopolavoro (OND)

Mussolini also wanted to bring the adult population of Italy closer to fascism. The Fascists introduced adult leisure programmes and facilities. These programmes were organised by the *Opera Nazionale Dopolavoro* (OND), established in 1925. It tried to attract ordinary people to fascism via subsidised activities such as arts, music, theatre and poetry. There were summer camps and sports facilities, as well as the provision of clothing for poorer people. Membership rose rapidly. Nearly every town had its own *Dopolavoro* clubhouse by the mid-1930s. It allowed the Fascists to manipulate public opinion and promote propaganda messages in a more subtle way.

Complete the table

Use the information on the opposite page to complete the table below summarising the nature and impact of Mussolini's policies relating to education and leisure.

Area	Key measures introduced by the Fascist government	How did these measures help to build support for the Fascist state?
Schools		
Universities		
Youth movements		
Adult leisure programmes		

Support or challenge?

Below is a sample exam question which asks how far you agree with a specific statement. Below this are a series of general statements which are relevant to the question. Using your own knowledge and the information on the opposite page, decide whether these statements support or challenge the statement in the question and tick the appropriate box.

How far do you agree that Mussolini's policies on education and leisure were successful in the years 1925–40?

	Support	Challenge
Some university lecturers refused to join the Fascist Party.		
Some university lecturers only joined the Fascist Party as a 'formality'.		
There was a significant increase in the number of students attending university.		
Membership of the *Opera Nazionale Dopolavoro* was high.		
Fascist education policy focused on indoctrination, rather than improving standards.		
The Catholic Church set up rival youth organisations.		
Membership of Fascist youth organisations fell sharply as soon as Mussolini was removed from power.		

Press control and censorship, propaganda, the cult of *Il Duce* and the influence of Fascist culture

REVISED

Like many other Fascist regimes, the Italian Fascists used a mixture of propaganda and control to make sure the population only received the messages the regime wanted.

Press control and censorship

Mussolini, a former journalist, knew how powerful the press could be. He took steps to censor and control it. The Press Law of December 1925 ensured that only registered journalists could write for the newspapers, and the Fascists controlled the registers. Editors who kept their jobs after 1925 knew that any opposition messages would lead to severe consequences.

Censorship was initially controlled by Mussolini's press office. This became the expanded Ministry of Propaganda in 1935, and was renamed the Ministry of Popular Culture in 1937. It introduced strict censorship of newspapers, radio, film, theatre and foreign publications. Newspapers were not allowed to publish anti-Fascist opinion or negative stories.

Propaganda

The Fascists used radio and cinema to promote their propaganda messages.

Cinema

The Italian Fascists took cinema seriously, building a school of cinematography in 1935. Film directors had a fair degree of freedom so long as they did not criticise fascism or the regime. In 1934, the General Directorate of Cinema was created, which regulated the cinema and brought all film in line with Fascist ideology. In 1938, the regime took over Italy's Hollywood, *Cinecittà* and after that it made several Fascist films. Films by the Fascist film agency portrayed current events, glorifying the regime and its successes. Everyone had to sit through these newsreels if they wanted to watch a film.

Radio

Radio was important because it could be received in rural and remote areas and did not require literacy. Radio became popular in Italy soon after its arrival in 1924–25. A special radio agency (the ERR) was set up in 1933 and was led by the PNF secretary. Mussolini expanded Italian radio during the Second World War and installed more than 2 million radio sets in marketplaces, schools, factories and military facilities. It reached a huge number of people and was an important channel of Fascist propaganda. Mussolini's major speeches were broadcast live and played via loudspeakers.

The cult of *Il Duce*

The Fascists tried to create a **cult of personality** around Mussolini, presenting him as a heroic, ideal leader. It aimed to ensure Mussolini's popularity and that of the regime. The media was actively used to promote the cult of Il Duce, and showed him as a man of energy and action. He was portrayed as the perfect role model for Italian men. Aspects that made him seem weak were never mentioned.

The cult of *Il Duce* convinced many Italians that there was no realistic alternative to Mussolini, and some became fervent fans. Others were more sceptical, although they tended not to express their opinions for fear of repression. Like with education, it is hard to know how genuine people's enthusiasm was for the cult of *Il Duce*.

The influence of Fascist culture

Mussolini used culture for propaganda purposes. In 1926, the National Fascist Culture Institute was established to spread Fascist culture to the masses. The Fascists wanted to create a new modern Italian culture based on the traditions of a more glorious past.

In art this meant looking to ancient Rome for inspiration or experimenting with modernist and abstract styles. Art frequently portrayed the people trying to make Italy a great nation.

The PNF also used architecture as a propaganda tool. Mussolini wanted to show how powerful his regime was and used vast modernist buildings to do this.

The regime was not very successful at creating a Fascist literary intelligentsia, as many writers remained disengaged from fascism.

Develop the detail

a

Below is a sample exam question and a paragraph written in answer to this question. The paragraph contains a limited amount of detail. Annotate the paragraph to add additional detail to the answer.

How far do you agree that Fascist control of Italy in the years 1925–40 was mainly the result of the use of propaganda?

Propaganda played an important role in establishing and maintaining Fascist control over Italy in the period 1925–40. The Cult of Il Duce was used to suggest that Mussolini was a heroic leader. In addition, the media was used to promote Fascist propaganda. Film production and screening was regulated. Furthermore, radio broadcasts were used to spread Fascist propaganda. Radio broadcasts were an effective means of spreading propaganda. Mussolini also controlled the press. In this way, propaganda was used to establish and maintain Fascist control of Italy in the period 1925–40 by encouraging people to see Mussolini as strong and dynamic and by exercising tight control over film, radio and newspaper production.

Add the context

Below is a sample AS exam question with the accompanying source. Having read the question and the source, complete the following activity.

Why is Source 1 valuable to the historian for an enquiry into the use of propaganda by the Fascist State in the years 1925–40?

First, look for aspects of the source that refer to the events and discussion that were going on around the time that the source was written. Underline the key phrases and write a brief description of the context in the margin next to the source. Draw an arrow from the key phrase to the context. Try and find three key phrases in the source.

Tip: look at the information above the source – you should contextualise this too. Pay particular attention to the authorship of the source and the date on which the source was written.

SOURCE 1

From Luigi Freddi, Director of DGC (General Directorship of Cinematography), 1937.

A nation that is able to avoid the harsher realities that involve all the world will be one where all the citizens, even the so-called private citizens, know how to think and act, not merely out of self-interest, but out of regard for the collective group, the nation ... The most powerful force, over the last three years, which has hastened the development of this attitude has been our film production. The new national film production is acquiring an international reputation and meaning because it expresses our time in history, which is truly Italian and Fascist.

Repression and terror

REVISED

After Mussolini had established his dictatorship, violence, formerly a constant feature of fascism, decreased as a way to maintain control. Repression was used in other ways. The police and local government had wide-ranging powers, and there was a climate of fear created by previous Fascist violence.

Role of the security services

The police, militia and security services were used to threaten, imprison and punish political opponents. Many political opponents were forced into exile and some were assassinated there. The attempted assassination of Mussolini in 1926 led to an increase in repression.

The Special Tribunal was set up in 1926 under the Law for the Defence of the State. These tribunals judged those thought to be a danger to the state. It met 720 times from 1927 to 1943, and considered 13,547 cases. As many as 5,155 people were found guilty and 49 were sentenced to death. Others were sentenced to house arrest or sent to prison.

The OVRA, or *Organizzazione Vigilanza Repressione Antifascismo*, was set up in 1927. This was a secret police organisation that had extensive powers to make arrests, hold people without trial, search people and places, tap telephones and intercept post.

The militia also helped to establish a climate of repression and fear. It was used to intimidate potential political opponents, assault those who were not co-operating and seize property.

The Fascists set up prisons in remote areas to house political opponents. Ten thousand people were sent there during the lifespan of the Fascist regime. This was not on the same scale as the Nazi concentration camps or the Russian gulags, but worked as an effective threat to those tempted to oppose the regime.

Anti-Semitic decrees

Italian Fascism did not have the same emphasis on anti-Semitism as in Nazi Germany. Some Fascists were anti-Semitic but this was not the norm. In 1937, the Italian Foreign Secretary, **Count Galeazzo Ciano**, did not support anti-Semitic policies and the regime even allowed 3,000 German Jews to enter the country as refugees from Nazi Germany. This changed suddenly in 1937. By 1938, anti-Semitic legislation was introduced and Jewish freedoms and living standards declined rapidly.

The development of the Italian racial laws, 1938

Date	Development
July 1938	The regime officially supported an anti-Semitic document called the 'Manifesto of Racial Scientists' which argued that Jews were not part of the Italian race.
August 1938	All foreign-born Jews were banned from state schools.
September 1938	All Jews were banned from state schools.
	Jews were banned from teaching in state schools; separate schools were established.
October 1938	Jews were excluded from membership of the PNF and other Fascist organisations.
	Jews were forbidden from owning large companies or landed estates.
November 1938	Jews were not allowed to marry non-Jews.
	Jews were excluded from the military and banking.
	Foreign Jews were expelled.

A consistent approach?

The Italian anti-Semitic laws were not consistently applied. Many government and Fascist officials did not apply the laws, either for religious or moral reasons or because they had close connections to Jewish families or friends. The anti-Semitic laws were unpopular with the majority of Italians, and academics, business elites and the Church spoke out against them. It lost the Fascist movement support from previously loyal people.

After 1943, when the Nazis returned Mussolini to power, he issued a decree to confiscate all Jewish property and round up all Jews. It was this action that led to the deportation of 9,000 Italian Jews to Nazi death camps. Only 600 survived.

Explain the difference

The following sources give different accounts of the impact of the Fascist use of terror in Italy. List the ways in which the sources differ. Explain the differences between the sources using the provenance of the sources and the historical context. The provenance appears at the top of the source in brackets. Make sure you stay focused on the differences that are relevant to the question.

How far could the historian make use of Sources 1 and 2 together to investigate the impact of the Fascist use of terror in Italy in the years 1925–40?

Explain your answer, using both sources, the information given about them and your own knowledge of the historical context.

Sources 1 and 2 disagree on the impact of the Fascist use of terror in Italy in the period 1925–40 because ...

SOURCE 1

Adapted from A Child in Confino *by Eric Lamet, published in 2010. Lamet and his mother were Jews sent by Mussolini's regime into internal exile (confino) in a remote village in southern Italy during the early years of the Second World War.*

The local official, Don Pepe, said to Mother, 'I will never understand why you people are being sent here. I think it is terrible that a fine lady like you should have to stay here. I'm supposed to make certain you follow all the rules set by those imbeciles in Rome. They also want me to read all the mail you fine people receive every day. Can you imagine? I should read all the mail of so many people. Only idiots can think up such foolish regulations.' It was obvious that he relished poking fun at the Fascist government. Mother said, 'How many prisoners are here?' 'About seventy', Don Pepe responded. 'All wonderful, cultured, and highly educated people.' He handed Mother the list of rules for prisoners and, from his expression of disgust, even I could tell he was not about to enforce any of them. 'But you will have to report to the local police twice daily', he added with a wink. 'If it were up to me, believe me ...' Holding his open hand level to his mouth, he gave his index finger a symbolic bite and threw the hand in the air. 'I have nothing to do with that.'

SOURCE 2

From Bread and Wine, *a novel by Ignazio Silone, published in 1936. Silone was a Socialist in exile.*

It is well known that the police have their informers in every section of every big factory, in every bank, in every office. In every block of flats the porter is an informer for the police. This state of affairs spreads suspicion and distrust throughout all classes of the population. On this degradation of man into a frightened animal, who quivers with fear and hates his neighbour in his fear, and watches and betrays him, sells him and then lives in fear of discovery, the dictatorship is based. The real organisation on which the system is based is the secret manipulation of fear.

AS-level question

How much weight do you give the evidence of Source 1 for an enquiry into the impact of the Fascist use of terror in Italy in the years 1925–40?

Explain your answer using the source, the information given about it and your own knowledge of the historical context.

Fascism and the conservative elites

REVISED

Mussolini attempted to reduce the power of the monarchy and conservative elites in order to gain more power for himself and the Fascists. He attempted to keep their support after gaining power so that it would be hard to challenge the regime.

The monarchy

The monarchy was important because of its connections to the judiciary, civil service and army. The Fascist State needed the support of all of these groups, and the King's support gave the regime legitimacy.

The King was not a strong supporter of fascism but did not oppose it either. He gained titles and lands from Fascist actions abroad. He signed most of Mussolini's decrees and did not try to curb fascism by using the army.

His power was reduced under the Fascist State. The Fascist Grand Council was given the power to fix the succession to the throne because the heir apparent had anti-Fascist sympathies. The King's command over the armed forces was transferred to Mussolini in wartime, and Mussolini did not ask the King's advice on policy.

King Victor Emmanuel III did resist some elements of fascism, for example those relating to the army, and refused to allow the Fascist symbol to be included in the Italian flag. He was critical of the anti-Semitic laws but still signed them. He had largely retired from public life by 1930, although he ordered Mussolini's arrest in 1943.

The judiciary

Anti-Fascist judges were removed from their posts and replaced with Fascists, meaning that the judiciary was under Mussolini's control. Imprisonment without trial became more frequent and Mussolini sometimes intervened to influence verdicts. Apart from the Special Tribunals, however, the system remained unchanged.

The Civil Service

Mussolini promised to make cuts to the Civil Service on coming to power. There were some cuts from 1922 to 1924 but otherwise little changed. By 1930, the Civil Service was expanding again. In 1935 membership of the PNF was made compulsory for civil servants, and the number of civil servants was greatly increased in order to offer jobs to Fascists.

Nationalists

Fascism stressed Nationalist themes in order to appeal to Nationalist groups, emphasising the importance of Italian culture and identity. From 1922 to 1924, Nationalists played a leading role in Italy's foreign policy, and Mussolini's attempts to increase Italian influence in the Mediterranean (in Corfu and Fiume) won him Nationalist support. In the late 1920s, Mussolini's involvement in the negotiations that led to the creation of the Locarno Pact, the Kellogg–Briand Pact (see page 72) and the Lateran Pacts (see page 64) won over Nationalists.

In the 1930s, the campaigns in **Abyssinia** (see page 76) and Albania (see page 78) were very popular with Nationalists as it led to the establishment of a new Italian colony and territorial gain. Outside of foreign policy, Mussolini's emphasis on Italian culture attracted Nationalists.

This led many Nationalists to support fascism until the Second World War, as it appeared to be committed to achieving Nationalist goals.

The armed forces

Mussolini attempted to appeal to the armed forces via the following policies:

- expansion of the armed forces
- aggressive foreign policy
- promoting senior generals.

Leading members of the armed forces gave Mussolini their support. Increasingly senior army positions were given to Fascists, to cement the loyalty of the army to the state. The armed forces were disunited and disorganised, and Mussolini never reorganised them. This ended up being disastrous in the Second World War.

Complete the paragraph

a

Below are a sample exam question and a paragraph written in answer to this question. The paragraph contains a point and specific examples, but lacks a concluding analytical link back to the question. Complete the paragraph adding this link in the space provided.

How accurate is it to say that the Fascist State had the support of the Italian elites in the years 1925–40?

The Fascist State had the support of the Italian monarchy to a fair extent. On the one hand, the King showed his support for the Fascist State as he signed the majority of Mussolini's decrees. In addition, he did not challenge a reduction in his own power. For example, he accepted that Mussolini did not seek his advice on policy making, and he agreed that the power to decide who succeeded to the Italian throne should be passed to the Fascist Grand Council. Furthermore, he did not try to use the army to restrict the power of the Fascist State. However, the King did resist some elements of fascism. For example, he refused to incorporate the Fascist symbol into the Italian flag, and he criticised Fascist anti-Semitic policy. In this way, ...

Extent of change

Below is a list of the people or organisations known as the conservative elites in Italy. Use your own knowledge and the information on the opposite page to reach a judgement about the extent to which the role of each changed under fascism. Write numbers on the spectrum below to indicate the relative degrees of change. Having done this, write a brief justification of your placement.

1 The monarchy

2 The judiciary

3 The civil service

4 The army

Little change ⟷ Significant change

Fascism and political and economic interest groups

REVISED

Central and local government

Mussolini centralised power in the years 1925–27. He did not share power with his ministers, who were meant to implement Mussolini's decisions obediently. Mussolini took the following key positions for himself:

- Head of Foreign Affairs
- Minister of the Interior
- Minister of all the Armed Forces

Centralisation

Mussolini quickly sidelined the Italian parliament (see page 44). In 1926, it lost its power to:

- discuss policy
- debate
- amend proposed legislation.

It became more irrelevant after all opposition political parties were banned and free elections ended. Parliament became full of Fascist supporters who rubber-stamped Fascist laws.

In January 1939, the Italian parliament was replaced by the Chamber of Fasces and Corporations, part of Mussolini's wish to establish a regime with power centralised in his hands.

Local government

Mussolini's determination to control the institutions of the state also had an impact on local government. Local self-government was abolished. Elected mayors and town councils were replaced by appointed officials known as *podesta*. They were chosen for their loyalty to the regime. The powers of Fascist prefects were also extended.

Mussolini's governmental system

Mussolini's governmental system was not efficient. He did not listen to advice, exploited rivalries in order to strengthen his own position and dismissed talented ministers because they questioned his ideas. Mussolini was poorly organised and bad at administration, which undermined his Government's effectiveness, particularly when he had so much control. He was successful in securing and maintaining political power, however, until the fall of the Fascist Government in 1943.

The PNF

When Mussolini became Prime Minister in 1922 he took firm control of the PNF. He rewarded loyalty and punished those who opposed him. After 1925, he took further action, closing the Party Congress in June of that year. In 1928, he purged the PNF, which was increasingly used for propaganda purposes rather than as a policy-making body.

Mussolini appointed people to positions who were obedient and unquestioningly loyal, which encouraged them to join the PNF to further their own interests. Men of ability were given posts where they would not pose a threat, which prevented the emergence of rivals to Mussolini. This was made easier by the divisions within the PNF, which meant that Mussolini could exert his dominance more easily. He manipulated different factions by appearing to identify with their interests.

Economic interest groups

Agriculture

The Fascists had always sought rural support, trying to appeal to rural employers and landowners. This continued after 1925. The Fascist Government continued to have close connections with southern landowners, who benefited from the ban on strikes and from the state-imposed wage controls because they could pay workers less. Landowners were also allowed control of policies such as land reclamation, choosing which land to be reclaimed. This meant that the policy did not have the intended radical effect on farming.

Industry

Mussolini tried to win over key financial and industrial elites. He created pro-business policies, for example:

- Telephone companies were privatised.
- Private life insurance was reintroduced.
- Taxes on 'excess' war profits were reduced or abandoned.
- Large firms and cartels were allowed to expand.
- In 1925, the Vidoni Palace Pact banned all Catholic and Socialist trade unions, leading to the banning of strikes.
- The bargaining rights of independent trade unions were removed.

These actions were crucial in gaining the support of industrial elites. Many businessmen were persuaded, and supported the regime. During the Depression the Government helped industry by supporting price fixing and cutting wages – this meant they kept the support of industry.

Simple essay style

Below are two sample exam questions. Use your own knowledge and the information on the opposite page and the previous page to produce plans for these questions. For each, choose four general points, and provide three pieces of specific information to support each general point. Once you have planned each essay, write the introduction and conclusion for the essay. The introduction should list the points to be discussed in the essay. The conclusion should summarise the key points and justify which point was the most important.

How accurate is it to say that the Italian elites benefited from the creation of the Fascist State in the years 1925–40?

'Mussolini was successful in his attempt to create a centralised state in the years 1925–40.' How far do you agree with this statement?

Spot the inference

High-level answers avoid excessive summarising or paraphrasing the sources. Instead they make inferences from the sources, as well as analysing their value in terms of their context. Below is a source and a series of statements. Read the source and decide which of the statements:

- make inferences from the source (I)
- paraphrase the source (P)
- summarise the source (S)
- cannot be justified from the source (X).

Statement	I	P	S	X
Mussolini called for illegal activities to end for there to be no more violence.				
Mussolini believed that the actions of the *squadrismo* could undermine his power and it should be disbanded.				
The Prefect represented the central government.				
Mussolini's system of government was inefficient.				
Fascist prefects had significant amounts of power.				
Mussolini sought to centralise power in Italy.				

SOURCE 1

From a message sent by Mussolini to Fascist prefects in January 1927.

I solemnly affirm that the prefect is the highest authority of the state in the province. He is the direct representative of the central executive power. Whenever necessary, the prefect must stimulate and harmonise the various activities of the party. The party and its members, from the highest to the lowest, now that the revolution is complete, are only a conscious instrument of the will of the state. Now that the state is equipped with all its own methods of prevention and repression there are some 'residues' that must disappear. I am speaking of *squadrismo* which in 1927 reappears in an undisciplined fashion during periods of public commotion. These illegal activities must stop. The era of reprisals, destruction and violence is over.

Economic policies

REVISED

In the early 1920s, Mussolini did not have a clear economic plan. As he became more secure in his position he became increasingly radical in his economic policies, resulting in the '**Corporate State**' in the 1920s and then **autarky** before the Second World War.

Early policies and the shift towards Fascist economics

By 1925, Mussolini had abandoned fascism's anti-capitalist ideas in favour of traditional economic policies which would attract the support of elites. These policies included free trade and *laissez-faire* economics.

Dramatic change?

During the economic boom from 1922, the Finance Minister **Alberto de Stefani** focused on the following:

- tax cuts
- pursuing pro-business policies
- reducing government intervention in the economy
- stimulating investment
- reducing public spending.

As a result, exports increased and industrial production boomed.

Shift towards Fascist economics, 1925–29

After de Stefani's removal in 1925, economic policy became dominated by Mussolini. In 1926, he aimed at economic self-sufficiency with policies such as the Battle for the Lira.

'Battle for the Lira'

In 1927, the lira was revalued from 140 lira to 90 lira to the British pound – meaning the lira's value would increase. Tariffs on imports were introduced, designed to protect the lira and the Italian economy. The Government became active in the following areas:

- regulation of industrial relations
- managing state finances
- further development and modernisation of the economy.

The revaluation undermined Italy's exports to some degree but made imports cheaper, which benefited industries that relied on imports. It led to wage cuts, falling living standards and rising unemployment. It did not lead to hostility to Mussolini, however, and propaganda focused on persuading the people to accept it.

The Corporate State

Under the Corporate State, workers, employers and Fascist officials were formed into corporations. They were to work together to resolve disputes between workers and management and to improve production.

The Vidoni Palace Pact, 2 October 1925

The Vidoni Palace Pact was signed between *Confindustria*, the industrial employers' association, and the Fascist trade union federation. Each side recognised each other as the only negotiator for their respective groups – other trade unions were excluded, and were dissolved after 1926. A Labour and Anti-Strike Law of 1926 banned workers from striking, and some professions were banned from being members of trade unions.

Ministry of Corporations, 1926

A Ministry of Corporations was established to oversee the new system. The corporations emerged slowly in the 1920s and were dominated by state-appointed officials. The system did not become fully operative until 1934. Corporations played a key role in labour relations and were glorified in Fascist propaganda, but were never fully supported by industrialists or Mussolini.

The trade union movement, 1927

Confindustria opposed all trade unions and were determined to retain control of their factories and businesses. In 1927, Mussolini broke down the confederation of Fascist trade unions into smaller federations. This reduced the influence of the trade unions in the workplace and boosted the power of the employers.

Success?

The Corporate State failed to have a dramatic impact on the Italian economy. It was used as propaganda but was effectively useless. Businesses ignored the regulations produced and maintained their own organisations, and the representatives of the workers generally sided with the employers. The Corporate State therefore did not result in an economic revolution.

Write the question

a

The following sources relate to Mussolini's economic policy in the 1920s and early 1930s. Read the guidance detailing what you need to know about Italy during this period. Having done this, write an exam-style question using the sources.

How far could the historian make use of Sources 1 and 2 together to investigate ...

___

___

Explain your answer, using both sources, the information given about them and your own knowledge of the historical context.

SOURCE 1

From My Autobiography *by Benito Mussolini, published in 1928.*

Amid the innovations and experiments of the new Fascist civilisation, there is one which is of interest to the whole world; it is the corporative organisation of the state ...

It was necessary to emerge from the base [selfish] ... habit of class competition and to put aside hates and enmities [anger]. After the war, especially following the subversive propaganda [of socialism], ill-will had reached perilous proportions. Agitations and strikes usually were accompanied by fights, with dead and wounded men as a result ...

The fact is that five years of harmonious work have transformed the economic life and, in consequence, the political and moral life of Italy. Let me add that the discipline that I have imposed is not a forced discipline ... and does not obey the selfish interests of classes. Our discipline has one vision and one end – the welfare and good name of the Italian nation ...

Instead of the old [trade unions] we substituted Fascist corporations ... We have abolished all ... [the] old troubles and disorders and doubts that poisoned our national soul. We have given a rhythm, law and protection to Work; we have found in the co-operation of classes the [basis] for our future power. We do not waste time in brawls and strikes, which, ... imperil our strength and the solidity of our economy.

SOURCE 2

Adapted from a lecture given by the exiled leader of the Italian Communist Party, Palmiro Togliatti, in Moscow, 1935.

The Fascist Party claims that Corporations were created to improve the living standards of the Italian people. This is a falsehood! Corporations were organised by the Fascist regime in Italy only after all democratic liberties had been denied. Corporations were only organised after the workers had been deprived of all representation, when all political parties had been destroyed, and when trade union freedom and freedom of the press had been crushed. Corporations were only created when every other possibility of expression for the Italian worker had been eliminated. Even if Corporations had some importance, they would not be able to do anything unless approved of by the Fascist Party.

AS-level question

How much weight do you give the evidence of Source 2 for an enquiry into the impact of Fascist economic policy on the lives of industrial workers?

Explain your answer using the source, the information given about it and your own knowledge of the historical context.

Response to the Depression, 1929–36

REVISED

The Great Depression prompted the Fascist Government to intervene more within the Italian economy. Mussolini promoted the Corporate State as the solution to the problems brought about by the Depression, although Italy suffered from those problems as well, including unemployment and an increase in the **balance of payments deficit**. In order to conceal this, the Fascist Government took measures to make it look like the economy was successful.

Measures to protect the economy

Italian banks had loaned money to industries that were now struggling to repay them due to a fall in profits. Mussolini's Government moved to protect the banks. In 1931, the *Instituto Mobiliare Italiano* (IMI) was established, and in 1933 the Institute for Industrial Reconstruction (IRI) was set up. They were established to rescue Italian industry and banks.

The IRI used state finance to buy worthless shares and lent money to industries that could be kept running. It also helped develop more effective management and mobilise resources more efficiently. The banking system became more or less state owned. Many small firms were saved from bankruptcy.

An Institute of Foreign Exchange was set up in 1934 to monopolise and regulate foreign exchange and currency trading, in order to maintain the value of the lira. Spending was increased on public works programmes and money was spent on welfare. These emergency measures were useful in preparing for the war against Abyssinia (see page 76).

Autarky

Autarky meant 'economic self-sufficiency'. As Fascist Italy was highly militaristic and nationalist, and aimed to increase its prestige abroad, war was ever more likely. Autarky was also introduced because of the League of Nations' sanctions on Italy following the Abyssinian War (see page 76). The High Commission on Autarky was established in 1937 to supervise the policies, but moves towards it had begun ten years earlier.

Measures taken to implement autarky included:

- the 'Battle for Grain'
- increased currency controls
- quotas on foreign imports, favouring domestic goods
- production of substitutes for substances not made domestically, e.g. lanital instead of wool
- searches for new energy sources that did not mean importing oil or gas.

The production of consumer goods was less of a priority and this helped to reduce the demand for imports, resulting in more finance becoming available to invest in military and industrial development. There were also negative side effects of autarky:

- Raw materials such as coal, oil and iron were very scarce.
- Domestic production of these resources met only one-fifth of Italy's needs.
- Wheat imports were cut by the 'Battle for Grain' but other food imports increased due to the concentration on wheat.
- Prices increased.
- Industries that were not prioritised suffered, e.g. textiles.
- Living standards of the peasants and industrial workers declined compared with the 1920s.
- When the Second World War broke out in 1939 Italy could not join the fighting because the shortage of foreign currency meant she could not import the raw materials to prepare militarily.

Establish criteria

Below is a sample exam question which requires you to make a judgement. The key term in the question has been underlined. Defining the meaning of the key term can help you establish criteria that you can use to make a judgement.

Read the question, define the key term and then set out two or three criteria based on the key term which you can use to reach and justify a judgement.

How accurate is it to say that Fascist Government policy <u>transformed</u> the Italian economy in the years 1925 to 1940?

Definition:

___

___

Criteria to judge the extent to which Fascist Government policy transformed the Italian economy in the years 1925 to 1940:

- ___
- ___
- ___

Reach a Judgement

Having defined the key term and established a series of criteria, you should now make a judgement. Consider how far the Government policy failed to modernise the Italian economy according to each criterion. You should refer to the information on the opposite page, the information on previous pages relating to Fascist economic policy and the information about 'The Battle for Grain' on page 62. Summarise your judgements below:

Criterion 1:

___

Criterion 2:

___

Criterion 3:

___

Finally, sum up your judgement. Based on the criteria how accurate is it to say that Fascist Government policy transformed the Italian economy in the years 1925 to 1940?

___

___

___

Tip: remember you should weigh up evidence of successful consolidation against evidence of limited consolidation in your conclusion.

The 'Battle for Births', the 'Battle for Grain' and the 'Battle for Land'

REVISED

The 'Battle for Births'

Mussolini launched the 'Battle for Births' in 1927, with the goal of increasing the Italian population from 40 million to 60 million by 1950. The intention was to build an increasing and youthful population to develop a strong Italian nation – to supply the army and govern its overseas empire.

The measures taken were as follows:

Rewards	Punishments
Loans were offered to couples who married, with part of the loan cancelled after every child was born, up to six children, when the loan was cancelled completely.	High levels of taxation imposed on bachelors for 'unjustified celibacy'.
Employment made more available to married men with children.	Bachelors were blocked from promotion.
A married man with six children was not required to pay tax.	In 1933, a quota was taken to limit the number of women in public sector employment, which was later extended to medium and large private firms.
Health provision for women and children was improved.	
Medals were presented to mothers who had large numbers of children.	

Despite all these actions, the marriage rate did not change and the birth rate was in decline until 1936. Women still made up 33 per cent of the workforce in 1936, a decline of only 3 per cent. The 'Battle for Births' therefore failed to achieve its key aims.

The 'Battle for Grain'

The 'Battle for Grain' was announced in 1925. Mussolini promised to make Italy self-sufficient in terms of grain production. Targets were set for increasing crop yields and high tariffs were placed on foreign imports. Grants were provided to farmers to use modern farming techniques and equipment. Marginal land was farmed to bring more land into production. This 'Battle' resulted in a 50 per cent rise in wheat production, especially in the Po Valley.

It was not completely successful, however:

- Valuable export crops such as olives and grapes did not receive the same investment, so did not match the progress of cereal crops.
- The rising prices in animal fodder meant livestock numbers fell.
- Although Italy became self-sufficient in crops it was not self-sufficient in fertilisers, which were necessary for high yields. When fertilisers could not be imported grain yields fell.
- Meat and egg production declined and imports of these foodstuffs increased.
- Prices rose and living standards declined.
- Government subsidies allowed inefficient farms to survive in the south.
- By 1933, Italy was still dependent on foreign imports.

The 'Battle for Land'

Mussolini's other main agricultural policy focused on land reclamation, known as the 'Battle for Land'. This was not a new policy in Italy but the Fascists aimed to do it on a far bigger scale. The 'Mussolini Law' of 1928 promised huge sums of money towards land reclamation projects. Any landowners who resisted would have their land confiscated. There would also be new irrigation systems, aqueducts, houses and roads.

This was a big success in some regions of Italy, for example Rome's *Campagna* district, and the Pontine where the main barrier to cultivation was drainage. In other regions it was a failure, however. Much land was untouched, and the scheme was badly administered. The number of poor families resettled on the land was tiny – fewer than 10,000. There was no genuine attempt at land ownership reform, which would really have improved the lives of the poor. In fact, the real wages of farmers fell by more than 50 per cent in the period 1926–34 and people continued to leave for the towns. This was in direct opposition to the Fascist aims.

Mind map

Use the information on the opposite page and the previous pages relating to Fascist economic policy to add detail to the mind map below.

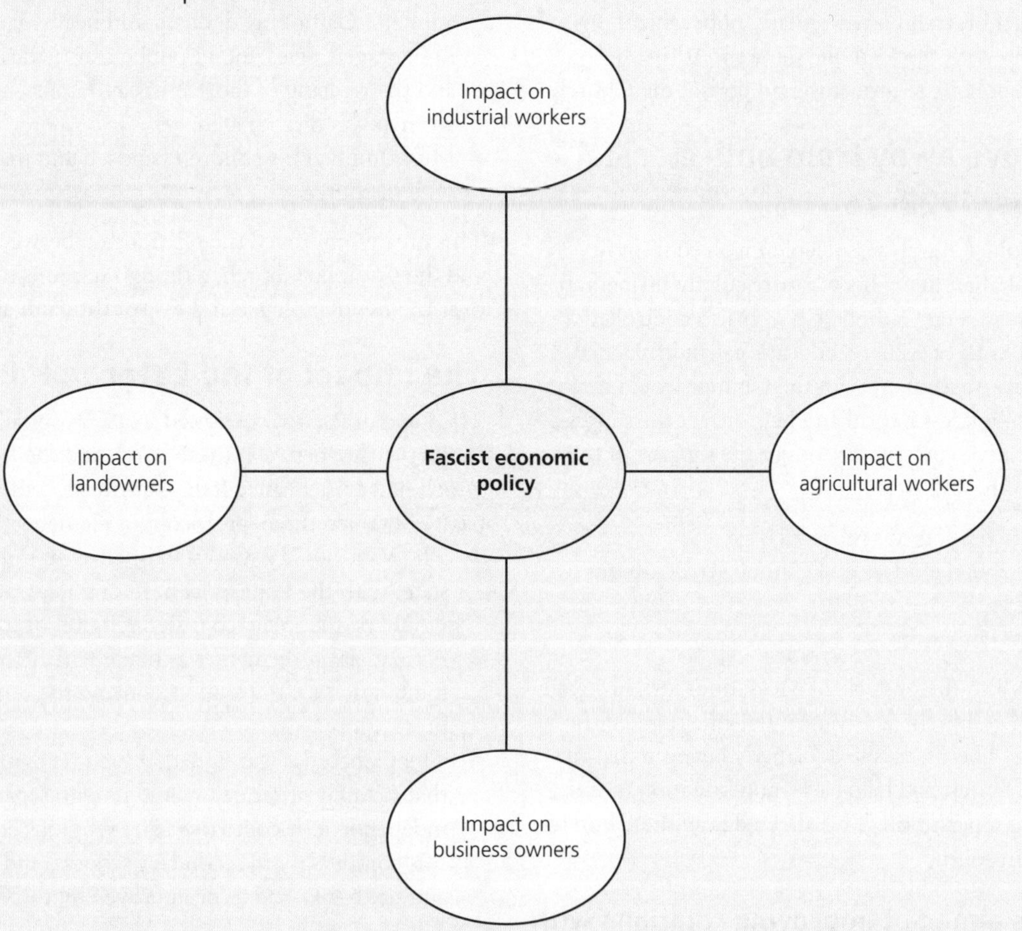

Delete as applicable

Below are a sample exam question and a paragraph written in answer to this question. Read the paragraph and decide which of the possible options (in bold) is most appropriate. Delete the least appropriate options and complete the paragraph by justifying your selection.

How far do you agree that Mussolini's social policies were successful?

Mussolini's Battle for Births was successful to a ***great/fair/limited*** *extent. The policy was intended to increase the Italian population by offering incentives to those who had large families, penalising men who did not marry and reducing the number of women in employment. However, instead of increasing, the birth rate declined in the period 1927 to 1936. Furthermore, the Battle for Births failed to reduce the number of women in the workforce. By 1936, women made up 33 per cent of the workforce, a decline of only 3 per cent since 1927. In this way, Mussolini's Battle for Births was* ***extremely/moderately/slightly*** *successful because ...*

Relationship with the Catholic Church

REVISED

Mussolini initially supported policies that gained him support, but became more radical as he consolidated his power. This trend is particularly noticeable in his relationship with the Catholic Church. At first he developed policies to attract the support of the Church.

The move away from anti-clerical policies, 1922–26

The Catholic Church was deeply involved in most aspects of Italian life. This was particularly influential in rural areas. The Catholic Church also controlled a strong network of welfare, educational and financial institutions. Agreement with the Church would make Mussolini look less radical and help attract the support of conservative elites, so he sought the support of the Church in the 1920s.

There were tensions on issues such as:

- the continued existence of Catholic trade unions
- education
- youth organisations.

There was also the obstacle of Mussolini's former stance towards the Church, as a committed atheist and critic of religion. The Fascists had formerly believed that the Catholic Church had held back modernisation in Italy, promoting superstition. This affected how the Church viewed Mussolini.

Policies aimed at improving relations with the Catholic Church

Mussolini was the first Italian leader to reach a clear agreement with the Catholic Church to reduce tensions between the Church and state. The following early policies helped to improve the relationship:

- In 1923, Mussolini helped to save the nearly bankrupt Bank of Rome, which managed the assets of the Catholic Church.
- Clergy salaries were increased and exempted from taxation.
- Mussolini granted 3 million lire to help restore damaged churches.
- Religious education was reinstated in elementary schools.
- The crucifix was restored to Italian schoolrooms and courts.
- Milan's Catholic university was given official recognition.
- Protection was given to religious processions.
- Mussolini tightened divorce laws, abortion was made virtually impossible and penalties were introduced for adultery. Gambling, dancing and heavy drinking were discouraged, swearing in public was made an offence and the wearing of short skirts and make-up by Italian women was discouraged.
- Mussolini had his children baptised and married his wife in church.

This greatly improved the relationship between Mussolini and the Catholic Church, although tensions remained over the use of violence and his **totalitarian** aspirations.

The impact of the Lateran Pacts

The Lateran Pacts were signed in 1929, signalling an end to the conflict between the Church and the Italian state which had existed since Italian unification in 1870. The pacts contained three 'protocols' or elements:

1. The Vatican City was established as an independent state, with the Pope as its head of state. Catholicism would be the sole recognised religion of Italy.
2. A financial agreement was made which compensated the Church for the land lost during the process of unification.
3. The Concordat was signed, which recognised that Church structures would remain separate and independent. It confirmed that religious education was compulsory in secondary schools, and teachers and textbooks had to be approved by the Church.

Mussolini also granted the Church the right to censor books, films and newspapers. The Pope agreed that the clergy would not join any political parties.

Benefits for Mussolini

- The Lateran Pacts were very popular, resulting in increased support for Mussolini.
- Limited concessions had been made.
- The Pacts brought international prestige.

Church support for the regime

The Catholic Church supported Mussolini because he was seen as an effective leader who could protect Catholicism from the dangers of socialism. The conquest of Abyssinia was seen as an opportunity to spread the Catholic faith. After the signing of the Concordat many members of the Church became active Fascists.

Qualify your judgement

Below is a sample exam question with the accompanying sources. Having read the question and the sources, complete the following activity.

How far could the historian make use of Sources 1 and 2 together to investigate Mussolini's motives for signing the Concordat with the Catholic Church in 1929?

Below are three judgements about the value of Source 1 to a historian investigating Mussolini's motives for signing the Concordat with the Catholic Church in 1929. Circle the judgement that best describes the value of the source, and explain why it is the best in the space provided.

1. Source 1 is not valuable to a historian investigating Mussolini's motives for signing the Concordat with the Catholic Church in 1929 because it was published in America, so the author may not have been in Italy at the time the Concordat was signed and it may be unreliable.
2. Source 1 is valuable to a historian investigating Mussolini's motives for signing the Concordat with the Catholic Church in 1929 because it reflects the view of an outside observer, who may be able to interpret events objectively.
3. Source 1 is valuable to a historian investigating Mussolini's motives for signing the Concordat with the Catholic Church in 1929 because it tells us that 98.28 per cent of Italians voted for Mussolini in the elections.

The best judgement about the value of Source 1 is:

____

because ...

____

____

Now apply what you have learnt by writing a judgement about the value of Source 2 for a historian investigating Mussolini's motives for signing the Concordat with the Catholic Church in 1929.

SOURCE 1

From an article in the American magazine Time, *published following the Concordat in 1929.*

Mussolini watched Cardinals and Monsignors marching to the ballot box, attended by blaring brass bands and wildly cheering throngs. Never before have Princes of the Church shepherded their clergy and people to vote in a parliamentary election. *Il Duce* has restored a mite of earthly authority to the Pope and last week we saw how mountainous is the Pope's gratitude to the Dictator. Pollsters estimated that His Holiness's influence had flung into the scale of fascism at least one million extra votes. Last week's election statistics prove that those Italians who went to the polls are 98.28 pure endorsers of the Duce.

SOURCE 2

From the 1939 revised edition of Mussolini's memoirs, My Autobiography, *Hutchinson & Co., 1939. Here, Mussolini reflects on the regime's 1929 concordat with the papacy.*

The so-called Roman Question embittered the souls of many Italians since the foundation of the Kingdom of Italy. People found it difficult to love one's country and pray to God with a clear conscience because it was the King of Italy who had robbed the Pope of his territories in 1870. Mussolini ended all that. He signed a treaty with the Pope on February 11th 1929 in which the old problem was laid to rest forever. There was great rejoicing.

Peace of heart of the Italian people was the result of this agreement. One could finally be both a good Italian, which is the same as being a Fascist, and a good Catholic. The Vatican itself found new dignity and new strength. The Lateran Treaty was, doubtlessly, one of the greatest achievements of the wise, realistic policies of Benito Mussolini.

Church–state tensions in the 1930s

REVISED

In the 1930s, Mussolini tried to make Italian society adopt Fascist ideals above all others. This led to growing tensions with the Catholic Church.

Catholic Action

The clash over Catholic Action was the first serious clash between Mussolini and the Pope. It took place in 1931, when the Fascist Government tried to suppress Catholic Action. The Pope criticised the move in an **encyclical** printed in foreign newspapers and the papal newspaper *L'Osservatore Romano* (see textbox).

A compromise was reached. It was agreed that Catholic Action youth groups would be restricted to religious, educational and recreational activities. The Church would still have a degree of influence over the youth. Membership of Catholic Action grew in the 1930s.

As part of this agreement, the Pope also emphasised that the Fascists must not persecute Catholic schools or interfere with either the Catholic university in Milan or the Federation of Catholic University Students.

Pius XI and the anti-Semitic laws, 1938–39

Pius XI had urged Mussolini not to introduce anti-Semitic measures in Italy, but Mussolini went ahead with his laws of 1938. Pius responded with public denunciations of the laws, declaring that Italy should not follow Germany's example of harsh and brutal anti-Semitic policies.

In 1939, Pius had prepared an encyclical letter which condemned racism, anti-Semitism and aggressive German nationalism, but he died before it could be published. His successor, Pius XII, chose not to publish the document. However, he did issue an encyclical shortly after the outbreak of the Second World War, using many of the arguments found in Pius XI's letter.

L'Osservatore Romano

This newspaper often reported and commented on political developments within Italy and abroad. The paper's blunt reporting and editorial criticisms of Mussolini's Government enraged Mussolini. However, although he threatened to shut it down, he never did so. During the Second World War, *L'Osservatore Romano* was the only Italian newspaper that published Allied war reports.

Support or challenge?

Below is a sample exam question which asks how far you agree with a specific statement. Below this are a series of general statements which are relevant to the question. Using your own knowledge and the information contained in this section of the book, decide whether these statements support or challenge the statement in the question and tick the appropriate box.

'Mussolini was successful in creating a totalitarian state in Italy in the period 1925–40.' How far do you agree with this statement?

	Support	Challenge
Fascist propaganda encouraged people to see the regime as strong and dynamic.		
From 1933, all teachers were required to be members of the PNF.		
Mussolini introduced strict censorship of newspapers, radio, film, theatre and foreign publications.		
Between 1927 and 1943, Special Tribunals considered 13,547 cases of people thought to be a danger to the state. Overall, 5,155 people were found guilty.		
King Victor Emmanuel III refused to allow the Fascist symbol to be included in the Italian flag.		
In 1926, the Italian parliament lost its power to discuss policy and debate and amend proposed legislation.		
Corporatism was used to extend state control over the economy.		
Mussolini's social policies – such as the Battle for Births – aimed to control aspects of people's private lives.		
In 1936, women made up 33 per cent of the workforce.		
The Lateran Treaties brought about a closer relationship between the Catholic Church and the Fascist regime.		
Membership of Catholic Action youth groups increased in the 1930s.		

Simple essay style

Below is a sample exam question. Use your own knowledge, the information in this section of the book and your answer to the task above to produce a plan for this question. Choose four general points and provide three pieces of specific information to support each general point. Once you have planned your essay, write the introduction and conclusion for the essay. The introduction should list the points to be discussed in the essay. The conclusion should summarise the key points and justify which point was the most important.

'Mussolini was successful in creating a totalitarian state in Italy in the period 1925–1940.' How far do you agree with this statement?

Recommended reading

- M. Clark, *Modern Italy 1871–1945*, Chapter 12 (1996).
- D. Evans, *Years of Liberalism and Fascism*, Chapters 8–10 (2003).
- R.J.B. Bosorth, *Mussolini's Italy: Life under the Dictatorship*, Chapter 9 (2006).

Exam focus (A-level)

REVISED

Below is a sample A-level exam-style question and model answer. Read it and the comments around it:

How far could the historian make use of Sources 1 and 2 to investigate Fascist attempts to indoctrinate the Italian population in the period 1922 to 1940?

SOURCE 1

Written by Luigi Freddi, the Director of the Fascist organisation the General Directorship of Cinematography, in 1937.

A nation that is able to avoid the harsher realities that involve all the world will be one where all the citizens, even the so-called private citizens, know how to think and act, not merely out of self-interest, but out of regard for the collective group, the nation ... The most powerful force, over the last three years, which has hastened the development of this attitude has been our film production. The new national film production is acquiring an international reputation and meaning because it expresses our time in history, which is truly Italian and Fascist.

SOURCE 2

From a July 1936 article by John R. Tunis, an American sports writer and broadcaster, entitled 'The Dictators Discover Sport'.

Mussolini had the idea of putting athletes to work in the service of the nation and of Fascist ideology by entering them in international competitions. Matches with other lands have become a powerful weapon in his service ... so in Italy victory over foreign lands becomes a salve, spread thickly on the national ego by the Duce. An Italian triumph in football, cycling, tennis, or any other sport, particularly if over old rivals like the French, is seized upon, written up and paraded as proof positive of the superiority of the race and its governing principles ... Italians and Italian teams about to go abroad are "pepped up" by interviews with Il Duce; they receive telegrams of exhortation before beginning their matches and messages of congratulation afterwards if they have done well. When the cycling team in the *Tour de France* placed up in front, Achille Starace, President of the Italian Olympic Committee and at the same time Secretary of the Fascist Party, sent a wire expressing the confidence of Il Duce and the country. In short, it is impressed on the Italian athlete that "he represents not himself alone but the entire nation in a struggle for the existence of a national culture." "Athletes of Italy," shouts Il Duce, "remember that when you fight outside the borders of Italy, you carry the honor, the sporting prestige of the nation in your muscles, your bodies and your souls."

Sources 1 and 2 are useful for an investigation into Fascist attempts to indoctrinate the Italian population in the period 1922 to 1940 because they provide contrasting views on the motivations for Italians to take part in sport and the film industry. Additionally, both sources were written at a time when such propaganda initiatives were at their height and well supported by both the Government and many of the people, particularly when their propaganda message was not too overt. In that sense they give a sense of the complicated nature of propaganda and its impact, as well as the range of ways in which the Government tried to send a Fascist message to the Italian people. In this context the sources are useful because they demonstrate the extent of the Nationalist and Fascist rhetoric in culture and sport in the 1930s, while raising questions about the purpose of such language.

> The essay starts by setting out a range of ways in which the sources might be useful for the enquiry the question focuses on.

Sources 1 and 2 are useful as they contain important views on the reasons why Italians were encouraged to take part in sporting competitions and watch or make new Italian Fascist films. According to Source 1, Italians were being strengthened as a nation by the film industry. Propaganda films were teaching their audience how to think, 'out of regard for the collective group, the nation'. Freddi believed that the films he helped to produce were creating a greater regard for the nation in a time of Fascist dominance. An 'Experimental Centre for Cinematography' was built

> This paragraph explains the way in which Sources 1 and 2 show the Government's desired effect of propaganda in the 1930s. In this way it discusses the sources in the context of their time.

in Rome in 1935 to train filmmakers, and the Italian Government was one of the first to take filmmaking seriously as a potential propaganda tool. Despite this, even though a General Directorate for Cinema was created in 1934 to regulate the cinema and bring all films in line with Fascist rhetoric, actually few overtly Fascist films were made before the Second World War. This makes Freddi's declaration less plausible in context. Source 2 agrees with Source 1 regarding the desired effect of the Fascist propaganda initiatives – to build a nation united under fascism, and a sense of shared superiority. In the light of other Fascist propaganda programmes, for example the rural radio agency (set up in 1933) and the *Opera Nazionale Dopolavoro* (1925), the sources' information regarding the Government's desired effect of propaganda is very plausible.

Here the essay integrates detailed contextual knowledge to evaluate the claims being made by Freddi about the influence of Fascist films.

Both sources were written at a similar point in the development of Fascist propaganda – Source 1 in 1937 and Source 2 in 1936. Cinema, radio and sporting successes were used at this point to raise morale and increase support for the Fascist regime. Mussolini's Government wanted Italians to believe that Italy was making rapid progress under the Fascists, and that the country was successful internationally and prosperous domestically. Source 1, therefore, speaks of the 'international reputation and meaning' of Italian film, and Source 2 of Italian sporting triumphs 'particularly if over old rivals like the French ... as proof positive of the superiority of the race and its governing principles'. Although Source 2 is from a hostile source, it was published at a time of sporting success for 'The Dictators' (Mussolini and Hitler) and although its attitude towards Mussolini's propaganda is fairly dismissive, its description of the Italian approach to sport in the 1930s is mirrored in the way that successes in the economy, culture and politics were celebrated by the Italian Government.

Sources 1 and 2 demonstrate the importance to Italian Fascism of using language related to strength and aggression. Both Freddi (in Source 1) and Mussolini (quoted in Source 2) talk about power and strength and being important to the Italian nation. Mussolini particularly emphasised the idea of a physical 'fight' in sport. Both sources show that Italian propaganda valued physical strength and aggression, and that this was one value that the Government wanted the population to absorb. This is particularly significant in the context of the militaristic nature of Italian Fascism, and the expansion of the armed forces by Mussolini.

This paragraph makes intelligent inferences based on the sources and contextual knowledge.

Overall, Sources 1 and 2 are useful because they take two different positions, and show how Italian sporting and cultural propaganda was particularly forceful in the 1930s, when Mussolini was trying to emphasise and improve Italy's international position. They demonstrate the value of physical strength and aggression within that propaganda and show that it was a central value of the Italian Fascist Government. Sources 1 and 2 are much less useful for showing how Italians responded to the propaganda. Source 1 is written from a government point of view, and Source 2, from an American author, would have had difficulty finding out how the audience reacted. It also only quotes Mussolini. Other sources are necessary to understand how successful these propaganda efforts were.

This paragraph summarises the argument of the essay and also discusses a prime limitation of the sources.

This is a strong answer. It interrogates the evidence of both sources with confidence. This is clear from the inferences it makes about the implications of Sources 1 and 2. It uses knowledge of the historical context to weigh the evidence of the sources and reach a judgement about the reliability of different aspects of the sources. The conclusion also discusses an important limitation of the sources, but the essay would have been improved by bringing this in earlier.

4 Challenges to, and the fall of, the Fascist State, c1935–46

Italy's international standing in 1935

REVISED

When Mussolini came to power he had certain foreign policy aims, including modernising Italy's armed forces and expanding her colonies in North Africa. He did not have a plan to achieve them, however. By the end of the 1920s, Mussolini was more secure in his power and became more adventurous in foreign policy.

Mussolini's foreign policy aims

Mussolini's early aims were to:

- achieve 'Great Power' status for Italy, making her an equal of Britain and France
- promote fascism and Italian prestige abroad, and gain colonial possessions
- establish Italian dominance in the Mediterranean, the Adriatic Sea and the Balkans, especially in Albania.

Problems with achieving these aims

In 1922, Italy had little influence on the international stage. Britain and France were still the key powers, they supported the Versailles settlement and both ruled over powerful empires. Italy could not challenge Britain and France in either military or diplomatic terms at this point. This did not stop Mussolini being determined to reverse the Treaty of Versailles, although he maintained good relations with Britain and France on the surface.

Mussolini's theory of encirclement

In Mussolini's speeches he both claimed friendship with Italy's First World War allies and denounced them as 'parasites'. He declared that he would destroy the British Empire and developed a theory that Italy was a prisoner in the Mediterranean, encircled by British and French military bases. This became the centre of Mussolini's foreign policy.

Mussolini and the search for allies

Strong alliances were necessary if Italy was to begin an assertive foreign policy. Mussolini signed treaties with many European countries in the early–mid 1920s. They were largely commercial treaties, though, and did not bring him the prestige he sought.

Mussolini had a reputation for switching allegiances when the circumstances suited him, so the treaties counted for little politically. Mussolini's search for allies had the reverse effect to that which he intended: he acquired a rather negative reputation as a politician as a result of it.

Mind map

Use the information on the opposite page to add detail to the mind map below.

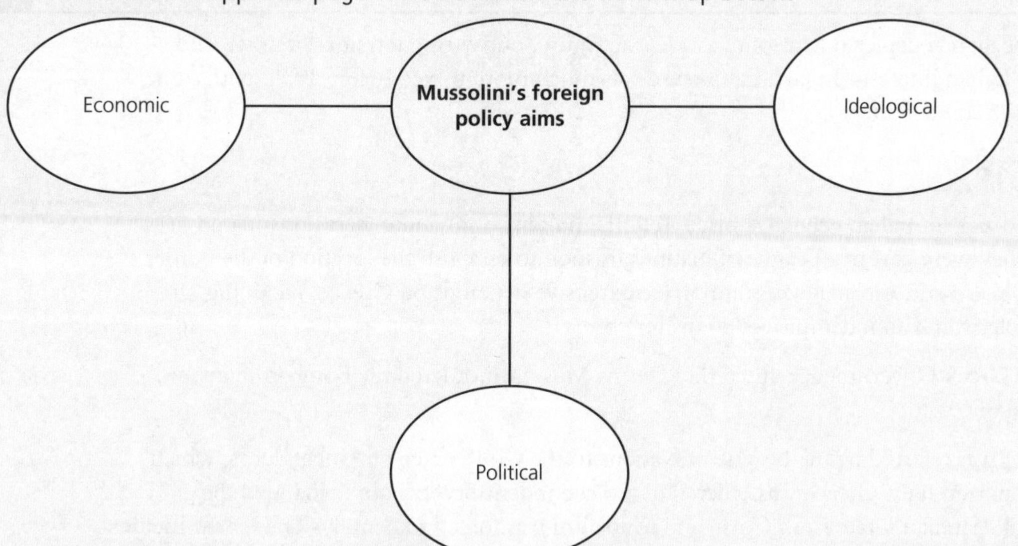

Select the detail

Below is a sample exam question with one of the accompanying sources. Having read the question and the source, complete the following activity.

How far could the historian make use of Sources 1 and 2 together to investigate Mussolini's foreign policy aims in the early 1920s?

Below are three claims that you could make when answering the question. Read the claims and then select quotes from the source to support them.

Mussolini hoped the success in foreign policy would help him to consolidate his power.

Economic problems also played a part in Mussolini's desire to form agreements with other countries.

Mussolini was willing to work with any country, as long as working with this country was of benefit to Italy.

SOURCE 1

From a telegram from Sir Ronald Graham, British Ambassador in Rome, to the British Government in January 1923.

To understand the situation here one must remember that omnipotent as [Mussolini] is, his position is full of difficulty and some striking success in foreign policy is of vital importance to him. He is having serious trouble with sections of his own followers. In any case, his foreign policy will be pure opportunism, and Italian friendship is on offer to the highest bidder. My impression is that he would prefer to work with Great Britain, at a price. It is a policy of sacred egotism carried to extremes. Possible economic necessities of Italy and those of his own political position afford some extenuating circumstances.

The impact of foreign policy success and failure before 1934

REVISED

Fascist propaganda depicted Mussolini as a heroic figure, outwitting foreign statesmen and defending Italian interests. In fact, the picture was much more mixed before 1934, with some successes and some failures.

Corfu, 1923

In August 1923, an Italian general, Enrico Tellini, and four of his aides were assassinated in Greece. They were part of a League of Nations mission to establish the location of the border between Greece and Albania. Mussolini made extensive demands on Greece, including an official apology and an indemnity of 50 million lire.

When the Greek Government refused these terms Mussolini ordered the bombardment and occupation of Corfu.

The matter was referred by the League of Nations to the Conference of Ambassadors, which largely supported Italy. Greece was ordered to pay the indemnity. Britain demanded the withdrawal of Italian forces from Corfu and Mussolini was forced to comply. The Corfu Incident showed Italy could not claim equal Great Power status. It revealed the constraints on Italian foreign policy, but also that international organisations could condone the threats of dictators like Mussolini.

The Balkans, 1924–26

When Ahmed Zog took power in Albania in 1924, Mussolini seized the opportunity to pressurise Yugoslavia into accepting Italian influence in the Balkans. He gave Zog financial support and in 1926 signed a treaty of friendship which confirmed Albania's position as an Italian **satellite state**. Albania bordered Yugoslavia, and Mussolini further destabilised Yugoslavia by supporting Croatian separatist groups and right-wing militias.

The Locarno Treaties, 1925

A conference of representatives from Britain, France, Germany and Italy was held at Locarno in Switzerland in an attempt to ease rising tensions in Europe. It proved very successful. Germany's western frontiers were confirmed, and the powers committed themselves to further work on settling Germany's eastern borders. Mussolini was content to work with the European powers, and Locarno presented Italy as a major European power.

The Kellogg–Briand Pact, 1928

In 1928, Mussolini signed the Kellogg–Briand Pact, outlawing war as a means to resolving conflict between powers. Nine powers signed the pact on 27 August 1928. A further 56 nations signed it afterwards.

Mussolini tried to use the pact as a chance to demonstrate his influence, attempting to persuade the delegates to travel to Rome to sign it. This proposal failed. The pact carried little weight with the powers, and Mussolini dismissed it in the Italian parliament shortly after signing it.

Spectrum of success

Below is a sample exam question and a list of general points which could be used to answer the question. Use your own knowledge and the information on the opposite page to reach a judgement about the importance of these general points to the question posed. Write numbers on the spectrum below to indicate their relative importance. Having done this, write a brief justification of your placement, explaining why some of these factors are more important than others. The resulting diagram could form the basis of an essay plan.

How successful was Mussolini's foreign policy in the years 1922–29?

1 The Corfu Incident
2 The extension of Italian influence in the Balkans
3 The Locarno Treaties
4 The Kellogg–Briand Pact

Less successful ←————————————————→ Very successful

Identify an argument

a

Below are a series of definitions, a sample exam question and two sample conclusions. One of the conclusions achieves a high mark because it contains an argument. The other achieves a lower mark because it contains only description and assertion. Identify which is which. The mark scheme on page 99 will help you.

- Description: a detailed account.
- Assertion: a statement of fact or an opinion which is not supported by a reason.
- Reason: a statement which explains or justifies something.
- Argument: an assertion justified with a reason.

How accurate is it to say that Mussolini's foreign policy was successful in the years 1922–29?

CONCLUSION 1

Overall, Mussolini's foreign policy in the years 1922–29 was only partially successful. He successfully extended Italian influence in the Balkans, and Italy's involvement in the Locarno Treaties and the Kellogg–Briand Pact indicated that Italy could work with the Great Powers in Europe. However, Mussolini failed to achieve 'Great Power' status for Italy, being forced by Britain to withdraw Italian troops from Corfu, and failing in his attempt to have the Kellogg–Briand Pact signed in Rome.

CONCLUSION 2

In conclusion, in the period 1922–29, Mussolini's foreign policy had some successes and some failures. The extension of Italian influence in the Balkans was a success, but the Corfu Incident was a failure, despite Mussolini being portrayed as a hero within Italy. In addition, Italy had signed two treaties, the Locarno Treaties and the Kellogg-Briand Pact. These treaties brought Italy into alliance with a number of other countries. In this way, in the period 1922–29, Mussolini's foreign policy had some successes and some failures.

Relations with Britain, France and Germany

REVISED

Relations between Fascist Italy and the other European powers wavered in the 1920s and early 1930s. Mussolini was torn between trying to maintain cordial relations with all the powers while having expansionist goals.

Britain and France

Mussolini was wary of straining relations with Britain and France. He portrayed himself as supportive of their interests. The following actions were intended to demonstrate this approach:

- Italy remained a member of the League of Nations.
- Mussolini signed the Locarno Treaties.
- He signed the Kellogg–Briand Pact.
- He reached agreement with Britain about colonial borders in North Africa.

Though Mussolini signed these agreements he was not fully committed to them, but was prepared to exploit the changing international situation to benefit himself and Italy. He hoped his actions would win him the favour of Britain and France, which would hopefully lead to concessions in Italy's favour.

Germany

In the late 1920s, Mussolini began to fund German right-wing political groups in the hope that a pro-Fascist government would emerge. He was aware that a strong Germany would act as a counter-balance to the power of Britain and France, and hoped this would make them more supportive of Italian aims in the Balkans and North Africa.

Relations were tense between Germany and Italy when Hitler came to power in 1933. Mussolini called for a Four-Power Conference in Rome between Italy, France, Britain and Germany following Hitler's withdrawal from the Disarmament Conference and League of Nations. Mussolini pronounced the conference a great triumph for Italy but it ended with no resolution, and Mussolini was still afraid that Fascist Italy would be subordinated to Nazi Germany.

Austria was on Italy's northern border, and Mussolini was concerned that Germany might seize any opportunity to annex the German-speaking state. He encouraged the Austrian Chancellor Dollfuss to clamp down on Austrian Nazis and create a regime based on Fascist principles. When Dollfuss was assassinated by Austrian Nazis in July 1934 Mussolini feared a German invasion of Austria. He sent 40,000 troops to the Austrian border to discourage Hitler from taking action.

The Stresa Front, 1935

Hitler's announcement in 1935 that Germany was developing her air force, introducing military conscription and rearming contravened the Treaty of Versailles. Mussolini called for a meeting with Britain and France to discuss these actions. The conference was arranged in April 1935 in Stresa, northern Italy.

- All three powers criticised German rearmament, which contravened the Treaty of Versailles.
- They agreed to co-operate to prevent any country from abandoning previously agreed peace treaties.
- They reaffirmed their support for the 1925 Locarno Treaties.
- They agreed to support an independent Austria.

Result

This was the high point of Mussolini's co-operation with Britain and France. The Stresa Front was vague, however, and did not include specific commitments for action from any power. They were not prepared to invade Germany to prevent further breaches of the Treaty of Versailles.

There was also division between the three powers on how to deal with Hitler. Britain undermined the pact when they signed the Anglo–German naval agreement in June 1935 without consulting France or Italy, and Mussolini used this as an excuse for abandoning it.

Complete the table

Use the information on the opposite page and your own knowledge to complete the table below indicating the extent to which Italy enjoyed good relations with the 'Great Powers' of Europe in the 1920s and early 1930s.

Country	Evidence of co-operation in Italy's relationship with this country	Evidence of tensions in Italy's relationship with this country
Britain		
France		
Germany		

Establish criteria

Below is a sample exam question which requires you to make a judgement. The key term in the question has been underlined. Defining the meaning of the key term can help you establish criteria that you can use to make a judgement.

Read the question, define the key term and then set out two or three criteria based on the key term which you can use to reach and justify a judgement.

To what extent was Mussolini's foreign policy successful in the period 1922–29?

Definition:

Criteria to judge the extent to which Mussolini's foreign policy was successful in the period 1922–29:

-
-
-

Reach a judgement

Having defined the key term and established a series of criteria, you should now make a judgement. Consider how far Mussolini's foreign policy was successful in the period 1922–29 according to each criterion. Summarise your judgements below:

Criterion 1:

Criterion 2:

Criterion 3:

Finally, sum up your judgement. Based on the criteria, to what extent was Mussolini's foreign policy successful in the period 1922–29?

Tip: remember you should weigh up evidence of successful consolidation against evidence of limited consolidation in your conclusion.

Foreign policy, 1935–40

REVISED

The invasion of Abyssinia and its consequences

At Stresa, Mussolini gained the mistaken impression that Britain and France would condone an Italian invasion and takeover of Abyssinia. There were several reasons why Mussolini was determined to launch a campaign in Africa:

- To satisfy Italy's Nationalist and colonial ambitions and increase the regime's popularity at home.
- To provide fascism with a major propaganda victory.
- To demonstrate to the world that Italy was a major power.

In December 1934, a military confrontation took place at the Wal Wal oasis in which 150 Abyssinians and 50 Italians were killed. Mussolini used the Wal Wal incident to prepare for the invasion of Abyssinia. He built up his forces throughout the summer of 1935 and had 220,000 troops on the Abyssinian border by October. The Abyssinian Emperor, Haile Selassie, sought support from the League of Nations, but the League refused to intervene.

Invasion, 1935

Mussolini authorised the invasion of Abyssinia on 3 October 1935. He hoped for a quick victory. Adowa was captured on 6 October, the site of a humiliating defeat for Italy in 1896. After this, however, the advance was slow.

In 1936, Italy finally won the war with a massive military build-up involving 600,000 troops and air power. The final assault on the capital, Addis Ababa, resulted in Selassie's exile and the end of the war on 5 May 1936.

It was trumpeted as a huge Italian victory and resulted in growing popularity for Mussolini at home. However, there were many negative consequences:

- The economic cost of the war was huge. It led to the devaluation of the lira, and reduced Italy's trade with Africa.
- Garrisons were established which occupied a large number of troops.
- Italy used mustard gas against Abyssinian civilians, which gave them a reputation for brutality.

Impact of the Abyssinian Campaign

Tensions grew with Britain and France. They did not want to push Mussolini towards Nazi Germany but recognised the need to prevent further aggression by him. They supported only limited sanctions against Italy. The Hoare–Laval Pact of December 1935 stated that Italy could retain most of Abyssinia but a smaller independent nation would be established. This was rejected by Mussolini and condemned in Britain and France. From 1936 onwards the relationship between Italy, France and Britain was arguably damaged beyond repair.

Intervention in the Spanish Civil War and its consequences

Mussolini decided to support General Franco, a fellow Fascist, who was involved in a civil war against supporters of the Spanish Second Republic. This was partly because France supported the Republicans and Mussolini wanted to gain more influence in the Mediterranean. He also did not want to seem subservient to Hitler, who also supported Franco.

He provided air, ground and artillery support for Franco, who defeated the Republicans in March 1939. The German and Italian military support was a key reason for this. Britain and France did not provide the Republicans with the same level of support. They refused to offer any official support and declared neutrality. Italy and Germany argued they were preventing the rise of socialism in Europe, as the Republicans received support from Stalin and the USSR.

Public opinion turned against Italy in western democracies. There was widespread sympathy for the Spanish Republican cause across Europe. Mussolini's relationship with Hitler and Franco severely damaged relations with Britain and France.

Franco's victory strengthened the position of Germany and Italy within Europe and weakened France and Britain. For Italy, the intervention had negative financial consequences. Much money was spent, Italian trade was disrupted and military strength sapped. Italy was involved in the conflict for a much longer period than Mussolini had hoped for.

Write the question

a

The following sources relate to the Italian invasion of Abyssinia. Read the guidance detailing what you need to know about the Italian invasion of Abyssinia. Having done this, write an exam-style question using the sources.

How far could the historian make use of Sources 1 and 2 together to investigate ...?

____

____

Explain your answer, using both sources, the information given about them and your own knowledge of the historical context.

SOURCE 1

Adapted from Carlo Levi, Christ Stopped at Eboli *(1945). Levi was a writer exiled to the south of Italy. Here he is describing the reaction of southern peasants to the invasion of Abyssinia.*

The peasants were not interested in war. War they considered just another inevitable misfortune. They were not afraid to go, but very few enlisted. It soon became clear that not only the purpose of the war, but the way it was being conducted as well, was the business of that other Italy beyond the mountains, and had little to do with the peasants.

October 3rd, which marked the official opening of the war, was a miserable sort of day. Twenty or twenty-five of the peasants, roped in by Fascist scouts, stood woodenly in the square to listen to the pronouncements that came over the radio.

The war so light-heartedly set in motion in Rome was greeted with stony indifference by these peasants.

SOURCE 2

From Mussolini's speech announcing the start of the Abyssinian War, October 1935.

Blackshirts of the revolution, men and women of all Italy, Italians scattered throughout the world, across the mountains, and across the oceans, listen! A solemn hour is about to strike in the history of the fatherland. Twenty million men are at this moment gathered in the squares throughout the whole of Italy. Never in the history of mankind has there been seen a more gigantic demonstration. Twenty million men: a single heart, a single will, a single decision. Never more than in this historic epoch has the Italian people revealed the force of its spirit and the power of its character. And it is against this people to which humanity owes the greatest of its conquests, it is against this people of heroes, poets, artists, navigators and administrators that they dare speak of sanctions.

AS-level question

How much weight do you give the evidence of Source 2 for an enquiry into Italian support for the invasion of Abyssinia in 1935?

Explain your answer using the source, the information given about it and your own knowledge of the historical context.

The move towards Germany

REVISED

The relationship between Italy and Germany was heavily influenced by the personalities of the two leaders. Mussolini admired and feared Hitler's growing power by the end of the 1930s, and Hitler influenced Mussolini's foreign policy decisions towards the end of the 1930s.

In 1938, Hitler carried out the *Anschluss,* the invasion and annexation of Austria. Mussolini's agreement to *Anschluss* in 1938 led to him losing popularity in Italy, despite it being obvious that Mussolini could not prevent Germany annexing Austria. It also led to Mussolini becoming the weaker partner in his relationship with Hitler. There were three main reasons why Mussolini and Hitler moved closer together by the end of the 1930s:

- The worsening relationship between Italy, Britain and France and the breakdown of the Stresa Front.
- The Italian economy became more dependent on Germany from 1936.
- By the end of the 1930s Mussolini was becoming more impressed by Hitler personally.

These factors resulted in the signing of the Anti-Comintern Pact on 6 November 1937 with Germany and Japan, a pact driven by a hatred of communism. These powers would become known as the Axis Powers, and made a formal alliance between Italy and Germany more likely.

Impact of the Sudetenland Crisis, 1938

In 1938, Hitler sought the return of the Sudetenland, given to Czechoslovakia in the Treaty of Versailles. This worsened European tensions. Mussolini recommended a conference in Munich between Britain, Italy, France and Germany to resolve the crisis. This provided Hitler with a diplomatic way to regain the territory, and the resulting agreement did this on 30 September 1938.

The Italian annexation of Albania, March 1939

In March 1939, Mussolini ordered the invasion of Albania. It was launched on 25 March and quickly defeated the small Albanian force. King Zog fled to London, and a Fascist regime was set up. As a result, Britain and France guaranteed military support to Greece and Turkey, convincing Mussolini of the need to draw even closer to Germany.

Domestic tensions

The alliance with Germany, the introduction of anti-Semitic laws and the possibility of war appalled the Italian elites and some Fascists. Anti-German feeling was reported among all social classes and the population was unprepared and unenthusiastic about war. The propaganda and military spending caused anger and ridicule, and Fascist squads were used to violently attack those who questioned the regime. Mussolini still remained relatively popular but criticism of the Fascist regime was increasing.

The Pact of Steel, 1939

The Pact of Steel was signed on 22 May 1939 and was a formal alliance between Germany and Italy. Hitler wanted the alliance because of his plans to invade Poland in 1939. The alliance would mean British and French forces remaining in the Mediterranean instead of fighting in Germany.

The pact committed Germany and Italy to supporting each other in time of war even if they had started the war. Effectively Italy was committed to following Hitler's foreign policy. After signing the pact Mussolini sent Hitler a message that Italy did not want to enter a war for at least three years. Hitler ignored this and invaded Poland in September 1939.

Italian neutrality, 1939–40

Italy remained neutral until June 1940. She was supportive of Germany's actions but was not prepared to join the fighting. There were several reasons why Mussolini chose neutrality:

- The Molotov–Ribbentrop Pact (August 1939) was a secret agreement between Germany and the USSR to divide Poland and avoid war for ten years. Mussolini portrayed this as a betrayal of the pact against communism.
- Mussolini was playing a waiting game – he did not want to commit to the losing side of the war.
- Italy was not ready for war – Italy's economy, industry and military were unprepared for war. Modernisation processes were incomplete.

You're the examiner

a

Below are a sample exam question and a paragraph written in answer to this question. Read the paragraph and the mark scheme provided on page 99. Decide which level you would award the paragraph. Write the level below, along with a justification for your choice.

How accurate is it to say that ideological factors were the main reason why Italy entered into an alliance with Germany in 1939?

In November 1937, Mussolini signed the Anti-Comintern Pact. This Pact was also signed by Germany and Japan and committed all three countries to work together to stop the spread of communism. In addition, in 1939, Mussolini and Hitler signed the Pact of Steel. This formed a military alliance between Italy and Germany, committing them to fight together in any future war. Mussolini signed the Pact of Steel because he liked Hitler and was impressed with Nazi Germany, because relations between Italy and France and Britain had deteriorated, and because the Italian economy was increasingly dependent on Germany.

Level: ☐ Mark: ☐

Reason for choosing this level and this mark:

____

____

Add the context

Below is a sample A-level exam question with one of the accompanying sources. Having read the question and the source, complete the following activity.

How far could the historian make use of Sources 1 and 2 together to investigate the reasons why Italy entered into an alliance with Germany in 1939?

First, look for aspects of the source that refer to the events and discussions that were going on around the time that the source was written. Underline the key phrases and write a brief description of the context in the margin next to the source. Draw an arrow from the key phrase to the context. Try to find three key phrases in the source.

Tip: look at the information above the source – you should contextualise this too. Pay particular attention to the author of the source and the date on which the source was written.

SOURCE 1

From the postscript to the diaries of Count Galeazzo Ciano, written on 3 December 1943. Ciano had been opposed to the Pact of Steel.

The decision to enter the alliance [the Pact of Steel] was taken by Mussolini, suddenly, while I was in Milan with von Ribbentrop*. Some American newspapers had reported that the German minister had been received in Milan with hostility and that this was proof of Mussolini's diminished personal prestige. Hence his wrath. I received by telephone immediate orders to accede to German demands for an alliance. That is how "The Pact of Steel" was born. A decision that wrought such a sinister influence upon the entire life and future of the Italian people was due entirely to the spiteful reaction of a dictator to the irresponsible and worthless utterances of foreign journalists.

*von Ribbentrop was the German Foreign Minister. He was meeting with Ciano to discuss a friendship pact between Italy and Germany.

The impact of the Second World War, 1940–43

REVISED

Hitler's *blitzkrieg* attack against France on 10 May 1940 was successful, and German forces made quick progress. Mussolini was frustrated by Italy's neutrality and decided that Italy would enter the war. This happened on 10 June 1940, for the following reasons:

- He feared Italy becoming a second-rate nation in a Europe dominated by Germany.
- Mussolini believed in war and violence as a way to achieve political goals and glorify fascism.
- Mussolini was a victim of his own propaganda and had to maintain the image of a man of action.
- It appeared that the Allies were close to defeat, and Mussolini wanted to make territorial gains.

Italy's entrance into the war was not welcomed within Italy or by Hitler.

Military failures in France, North Africa and the Mediterranean

The Italian army suffered a series of humiliations rather than glorious victories. Italy was the minor partner in the Axis alliance.

France

On 21 June 1940, France declared an armistice with Nazi Germany, and Italy launched an offensive along the Alpine front. Italy's army only advanced a few miles before stalling due to resistance by French troops. The armistice was signed on 22 June. Mussolini hoped to gain a lot of territory but was not invited to the armistice. Italy received only a small amount of territory – two small towns.

North Africa

Mussolini was affronted at the insignificant gains from the French offensive. He tried to make gains in North Africa, ignoring the advice of his generals and invading British Somaliland. Troops were also sent into Egypt and towards the Suez Canal in September 1940. This inevitably prompted a counter-attack, one that was devastating to Italian forces. British forces advanced and took territory in Libya and by April 1941 took Abyssinia. One hundred and twenty five thousand Italian soldiers were taken prisoner and German forces had to be sent in to retrieve the situation.

Despite the arrival of German forces, the Axis powers were on the retreat in North Africa in 1942. They surrendered on 12 May 1943, paving the way for the Allied invasion of Sicily two months later.

The Mediterranean

Mussolini's failure to act decisively in the Mediterranean highlighted the weaknesses of the Italian navy and air force:

- Gibraltar was an important choke point for Britain in the Mediterranean. Even after Britain's land forces were ejected from Europe in 1940, Italy was reluctant to take action to secure the colony.
- Malta posed a constant threat of a close blockade of southern Italy by British naval and air bases. Italian forces had not had sufficient training to launch an amphibious attack on the island. Malta also threatened Italy's supply lines with Libya.
- In 1940, Mussolini refused Hitler's offer of the French colony of Tunisia, fearing that Italy would be dragged into a prolonged campaign by the French colonial authorities.

Disaster in Greece

Mussolini decided to use Albania as a base to invade Greece and gain some more territory. He did not inform Hitler as he saw the Balkans as his own sphere of influence. On 26 October 1940, Mussolini's ambassador presented Greece with an ultimatum – to grant Italy the right to occupy areas of Greece in exchange for Italian neutrality. Unsurprisingly, Greece rejected the offer. On 28 October 1940, therefore, 70,000 Italian troops invaded Greece from Albania.

The invasion did not proceed as planned. The Italian commanders thought it would take only two weeks to occupy Greece but the army was too small and poorly led. While the Greek army was small it was determined and knew the territory well. They offered significant resistance, pushing the campaign into the winter. Many Italian soldiers surrendered, and a Greek counter-attack in December 1940 drove the Italians back into Albania. A spring offensive made little progress, as did massive reinforcements. The British navy inflicted another crushing defeat on the Italian navy at Cape Matapan in March 1941.

The Greek campaign made Italy a laughing stock around Europe and drew Hitler's disapproval. In spring 1941, Germany invaded and took over Greece and Yugoslavia. Both countries surrendered by May 1941. The Balkan coast was under German control and Italy was clearly the junior partner once again in the Axis alliance.

Identify key terms

Below is a sample exam question which includes a key word or term. Key terms are important because their meaning can be helpful in structuring your answer, developing an argument and establishing criteria that will help form the basis of a judgement.

How accurate is it to say that Italian foreign policy became increasingly aggressive in the period 1922–43?

- First, identify the key word or term. This will be a word or phrase that is important to the meaning of the question. Underline the word or phrase.
- Second, define the key phrase. Your definition should set out the key features of the phrase or word that you are defining.
- Third, make an essay plan that reflects your definition.
- Finally, write a sentence answering the question that refers back to the definition.

Now repeat the task, and consider how the change in key terms affects the structure, argument and final judgement of your essay.

How accurate is it to say that Italian foreign policy became increasingly unsuccessful in the period 1922–43?

Support your judgement

Below are a sample exam question and two basic judgements. Read the exam question and the two judgements. Support the judgement that you agree with most strongly by adding a reason that justifies the judgement.

'Mussolini's foreign policy failed to meet its aims in the period 1922–43.' How far do you agree with this statement?

Overall, Mussolini's foreign policy did meet its aims in the period 1922–43.

____

____

Mussolini's foreign policy did not meet its aims in the period 1922–43.

____

____

Tip: whichever option you choose you will have to weigh up both sides of the argument. You could use words such as 'whereas' or 'although' in order to help the process of evaluation.

War economy and military weakness

REVISED

In 1940, the Italian economy and military were unprepared for war. The army was poorly equipped, undermanned and badly commanded, and there were shortages of fuel and ammunition. Furthermore, Allied bombing raids into northern Italy dramatically dented industrial production.

Italy's economy was not geared towards war production. Italy's proportion of gross domestic product (GDP) directed towards war production never exceed 25 per cent. This strongly contrasted with Germany, where the figure was 64 per cent. As a result, weapons, clothing and food were in short supply. It meant smaller British forces could defeat substantial Italian armies.

Fascist Italy had failed to develop an efficient centralised economy directed towards efficient war production. The bureaucratic system was poorly led, inefficient and corrupt. There was no economic reorganisation and vital war materials had not been stockpiled prior to June 1940.

The Italians depended almost entirely on German coal for fuel due to a shortage of oil imports. Germany could only send 1 million tonnes of coal per month, and many Italian factories lacked basic raw materials. This led to a poor rate of weapon and ammunition production. Steel production even fell in wartime. By 1942, a better level of arms production was achieved but this was then destroyed in Allied bombing raids which began in the autumn of 1942.

Italy's military weaknesses

Italy's military forces had many different weaknesses:

General weakness	Specifics
Command structures	There were no unified lines of command and a limited hierarchy below Mussolini. This led to a lack of co-ordination with disastrous results.
Mussolini	He insisted on being involved with strategy and command but made disastrous and ill-informed decisions. He had little experience of war or foreign policy, and failed to establish a coherent strategy.
Training	The military academies were outdated and field officers poorly trained. The training they had was obsolete.
Lack of strategy	There was an overall lack of planning or strategy.
Poor morale	The army was used to losing by spring 1941, and although the soldiers fought with courage they were badly supplied and equipped, not to mention unenthusiastic about the cause.
Equipment	Weapons were inadequate. There were only enough weapons to arm half of the units, and due to the lack of planning the artillery was often sent to the wrong place. The army was largely an infantry army, often using the same equipment as in the First World War.
Supplies	Clothing and food rations were inadequate. The rations were low, and the clothing supplied was worse than in the First World War.

Develop the detail

a

Below is a sample exam question and a paragraph written in answer to this question. The paragraph contains a limited amount of detail. Annotate the paragraph to add additional detail to the answer.

To what extent was the Second World War the main reason for the collapse of fascism in Italy?

Italian military weaknesses during the Second World War played a significant role in bringing about the collapse of fascism in Italy. For example, Mussolini insisted on being involved in key decision making. In addition, the weapons provided were inadequate. Finally, training of soldiers was inadequate. In this way, Italian military weaknesses during the Second World War played a significant role in bringing about the collapse of fascism in Italy because soldiers felt let down by Mussolini and his Government, and sought an alternative.

Introducing an argument

Below are a sample exam question, a list of key points to be made in the essay and a simple introduction and conclusion for the essay. Read the question, the plan, and the introduction and conclusion. Rewrite the introduction and the conclusion in order to develop an argument.

To what extent was Mussolini's foreign policy in the years 1922–43 a failure?

Key points

- The Corfu Incident
- The extension of Italian influence in the Balkans
- Signing of the Locarno Pact and the Kellogg–Briand Pact
- The Abyssinian Campaign
- Involvement in the Spanish Civil War
- The Pact of Steel
- Italian involvement in the Second World War

Introduction

There were seven significant events in Italian foreign policy in the period 1922–43. These were the Corfu Incident, the extension of Italian influence in the Balkans, the signing of the Locarno Pact and the Kellogg–Briand Pact, the Abyssinian Campaign, involvement in the Spanish Civil War, the Pact of Steel and Italian involvement in the Second World War. Some of these events were failures, but some were successes.

Conclusion

In conclusion, in some ways Italian foreign policy in the period 1922–43 was a failure and in some ways it was a success.

Political tensions in 1943

REVISED

Italy's entry into the Second World War led to increasing opposition to Mussolini and fascism.

Causes of political tensions

From late 1942, disillusion with, and opposition to, Mussolini and the Fascist regime grew dramatically. Allied bombing raids took their toll on national morale. Protests turned into political and anti-Fascist demonstrations. When the Government restricted an evacuation allowance to heads of families only, 100,000 workers went on strike for a week in March 1943, the most significant series of strikes since 1925.

Workers began to protest openly about their working conditions. These were fuelled by longer working hours, more stringent working conditions and increased bombing raids on factories. The strikes in March 1943 marked the start of more organised opposition to the regime. Moreover, many factories were at a standstill because of a lack of fuel and raw materials.

Declining living standards were an important reason for opposition to the Fascist regime. Food shortages were endemic, and prices rose to unprecedented levels. Groups that had been historically opposed to fascism, for example Catholics, Socialists and supporters of democracy, saw a chance to attract support and oppose the regime. Socialist and communist groups, encouraged by the extent of the Milan strikes, grew in numbers and influence. The Fascist propaganda machine began to fall apart in 1943 as an increasing number of people listened to the news from trusted sources such as Britain's world service and the Vatican's radio service.

Other factors added to the political and social crisis facing the regime in 1943:

- Returning soldiers with tuberculosis brought news of the conditions at the front line, adding to the anger and disillusionment of the population.
- The loss of 200,000 Italian soldiers at Stalingrad infuriated Italians who saw that as Germany's war. Additionally, skilled Italian workers had been sent to work in German factories.
- Many Italians were opposed to the brutal methods used by German forces in Greece and Yugoslavia.
- Younger Fascists were angered by the exemption of senior PNF men from military service, and criticism of corruption and inefficiency increased.

As a result, PNF party numbers fell dramatically.

By mid-July 1943, Italy was close to military defeat. Allied forces had landed in Sicily and were making rapid advances against both Italian and German forces. Mussolini blamed a range of people for this, from various Italian generals to Hitler. Most Italians, however, saw Mussolini as the reason for their problems. They were convinced that the war had been lost, and they wanted to abandon the German alliance, remove Mussolini from power and reach a peace agreement with the Allies. By 1943, this view was also held by leading Italian Fascists.

Venn diagram

Use the information in this section so far to add detail to the Venn diagram below. On one side of the diagram, list the foreign policy initiatives that increased Mussolini's popularity in Italy. On the other side of the diagram, list the foreign policy initiatives that decreased Mussolini's popularity in Italy. In the centre, list the foreign policy initiatives that had a mixed effect on Mussolini's popularity.

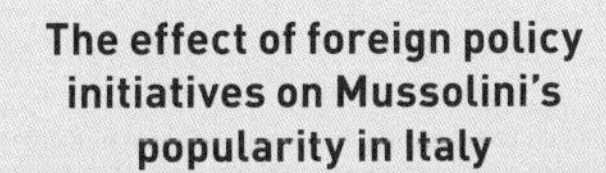

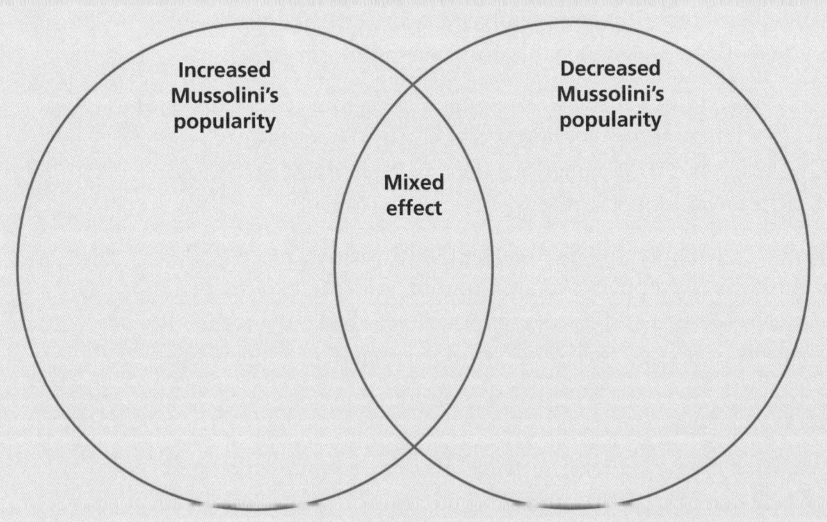

Identify the concept

a

Below are five sample exam questions based on some of the following concepts:

- Cause questions concern the reasons for something, or why something happened.
- Consequence questions concern the impact of an event, an action or a policy.
- Change/continuity questions ask you to investigate the extent to which things changed or stayed the same.
- Similarity/difference questions ask you to investigate the extent to which two events, actions or policies were similar.
- Significance questions concern the importance of an event, an action or a policy.

Read each of the questions and work out which of the concepts they are based on.

How accurate is it to say that Italian foreign policy became increasingly aggressive in the period 1922–43?

To what extent was Mussolini's foreign policy successful in the period 1922–29?

'Fascist Italy failed because Mussolini's foreign policy aims were too ambitious.' How far do you agree with this statement?

How accurate is it to say that public dissent played a fundamental role in the collapse of fascism in Italy in 1943?

How far can the Italian involvement in the Second World War be described as a complete disaster?

The Allied invasion and the removal of Mussolini, July 1943

REVISED

Allied forces landed in Sicily on 10 July 1943. They hoped the invasion would lead to the collapse of the Italian Fascist regime and the withdrawal of Italy from the war. US forces were led by Lieutenant General Patton and General Montgomery led the British ground forces. The main forces landed in Sicily. British and American soldiers drove the German and Italian troops from Sicily after 38 days of fighting. The Italian mainland was now under serious threat of invasion and defeat seemed inevitable for Italy.

Allied troops encountered only light resistance. Hitler had only left two German divisions in Sicily, and the defence was also weakened by German and Italian losses in North Africa.

The Allied invasion of Sicily fatally undermined the Fascist regime. On 25 July 1943, Mussolini was deposed and arrested and the first Italian troops withdrew from Sicily. Hitler instructed German forces to make withdrawal plans but also to continue their fierce resistance to Allied attacks. Axis troops were driven back towards the north-eastern corner of Sicily.

As Allied forces closed in on the port of Messina, the German and Italian armies successfully evacuated 100,000 men and various vehicles, supplies and ammunition to the Italian mainland. On 17 August 1943, US forces entered Messina and discovered Axis forces had evacuated. This undermined the Allied victory, but the next stage was to invade the mainland in September.

Mussolini deposed, July 1943

Mussolini's removal was partly caused by King Victor Emmanuel III. He was pressurised into action by frustrated Italian generals. It was also partly caused by opposition to Mussolini from within the Fascist Grand Council. This was significant since they had been selected for their loyalty and had never seriously threatened his position before.

In 1943, Mussolini announced his intention of holding a meeting of the Grand Council. It had not met since the beginning of the Second World War. He hoped to pressurise its members to declare their support for him and his policies.

Leading Fascists such as **Dino Grandi** saw this as an opportunity to remove Mussolini. The military defeats and subservient relationship to Germany had made them lose faith in Mussolini as leader. Grandi, Guiseppe Bottai and Count Galeazzo Ciano aimed to persuade the other Grand Council Members to support Grandi's resolution that the Council had lost confidence in Mussolini as Fascist leader of Italy. The King would become the head of the Grand Council and parliament.

The meeting was held on 24 July. Mussolini seemed to be taken by surprise during the meeting, especially when the Council voted 19 to 7 to support Grandi's resolution. Mussolini initially ignored the vote and met with the King on 25 July. He intended to intimidate the King into supporting him.

During the meeting the King informed Mussolini that he believed the war was lost, and that Mussolini had been replaced as Prime Minister by Marshal Badoglio. He was then arrested and taken away as a prisoner. Mussolini was liberated in a daring raid by German paratroopers on 12 September 1943 and placed in charge of the **Republic of Salò**.

Qualify your judgement

Below is a sample A-level exam question with one of the accompanying sources. Having read the question and the source, complete the following activity.

How far could the historian make use of Sources 1 and 2 together to investigate the reasons why Mussolini fell from power in July 1943?

Below are three judgements about the value of Source 1 to a historian investigating the reasons why Mussolini fell from power. Circle the judgement that best describes the value of the source, and explain why it is the best in the space provided.

1. Source 1 is not valuable to a historian investigating the reasons why Mussolini fell from power because it is written by someone who supported the attempt to remove Mussolini from power, and therefore it is biased.
2. Source 1 is partially valuable to a historian investigating the reasons why Mussolini fell from power because it summarises the view of a leading Fascist, who was well placed to understand the deficiencies of Mussolini's leadership. However, the speech described was given to persuade Grand Council members to support the motion to remove Mussolini from power, and therefore it may not provide an entirely accurate account of Mussolini's weaknesses.
3. Source 1 is valuable to a historian investigating the reasons why Mussolini fell from power because it summarises the view of a leading Fascist, who was well placed to understand the deficiencies of Mussolini's leadership.

The best judgement about the value of Source 1 is:

____

because ...

____

____

AS-level question

How much weight do you give to the evidence of Source 1 for an enquiry into the reasons why Mussolini fell from power in 1943?

Explain your answer using the source, the information given about it and your own knowledge of the historical context.

SOURCE 1

From Luigi Federzoni's summary of the speech made by Dino Grandi to the Grand Council of Fascism on 25 July 1943. Federzoni supported Grandi's attempt to remove Mussolini from power.

The Head of government, Grandi observed, has spoken of the unpardonable errors committed by military leaders and by the armed forces that he personally commands. But Mussolini, Head of government and the minister in charge of all the armed services, has had seventeen years to create, organise, prepare and to select the officer corps, the troops and the equipment ... Military preparedness was therefore the major task for the man who had the honour of guiding the destiny of the nation. The Grand Council must decide that the regime of dictatorship is over because it has compromised the vital interests of the nation, has brought Italy to the brink of military defeat and has damaged the revolution and fascism itself. The Grand Council must decide to restore all the authority and responsibility of state institutions which the dictatorship has absorbed and return to the Crown, the Grand Council, the Parliament and the corporations all the tasks assigned to them by our constitutional laws.

Democracy restored, 1943–46

REVISED

The Allied invasion, the Republic of Salò and the Government in the south

Following the invasion of Sicily, the Allies planned to invade mainland Italy. This, alongside Mussolini's rescue by German paratroopers, led to the establishment of two separate Governments in Italy.

The Allied invasion

American troops landed on the Italian coast at Salerno on 9 September 1943. The German army nearly succeeded in pushing back US forces. They halted the Allied army advance for four months. It took Allied soldiers four gruelling battles over several months to break through heavily fortified Monte Cassino and the Gustav Line of German defence. This was finally achieved in May 1944. The German commander, Field Marshal Kesselring, managed to organise a successful retreat of most of his army, which prolonged fighting further.

American forces entered Rome on 4 June 1944, but the D-Day landings in Normandy were scheduled for 6 June and this took priority over the Italian campaign. Six Allied divisions were removed from Italy as a result of D-Day, and heavy rain further delayed advances.

The priority for the Allied High Command was to keep as many German divisions in Italy as long as possible rather than to achieve a rapid victory, which meant the war in Italy was brutal and protracted.

Northern Italy became the scene of a vicious civil war between Italian Fascists and **partisans** who were determined to destroy the Fascist regime.

The Republic of Salò

The Italian Social Republic, commonly referred to insultingly as the Republic of Salò, was established by the Nazis in northern Italy with Mussolini at its head. There was no clear central authority for the Republic of Salò. Hitler would not let Mussolini establish a central government in Milan because of fears he would develop an effective power base and threaten German interests in Italy. Rome was made the official capital even though it was not under Mussolini's control.

The republic only lasted 600 days. Mussolini was both Head of State and Foreign Minister, and refused to recognise the authority of the Italian King. Various government departments were established under loyal Fascists, and the PNF was replaced by the Republican Fascist Party. The small membership of this party shows how unpopular fascism was after 1943.

The republic had an army, navy and air force, which fought alongside German forces with around 50,000 men. Fear and oppression was used to 'encourage' participation. There was a Fascist police force and militia, who played a key role in fighting partisans.

All those who voted for Grandi's motion on 25 July (see page 86) were condemned to death and five were executed – including Mussolini's son-in-law Count Galeazzo Ciano.

The power of the Salò Republic was very limited for the following reasons:

- Many Italians had lost faith in Mussolini and the Fascists.
- The Republic heavily depended on German support.
- Mussolini was treated as a puppet leader by the Germans.
- Mussolini had lost his charisma and was suffering from ill health.
- By 1944, the partisans posed a serious threat to German forces and the Salò Republic.

The Government in the south

The part of Italy ruled by the King and Provisional Government was small. The Allies directly ruled Sicily and most of southern Italy as the Allied Military Government (AMG). The Provisional Government controlled Sardinia and four south-eastern provinces. The Government had minimal influence, even after the signing of an Armistice on 8 September 1943. It barely had an army. It was initially led by Marshal Badoglio, who was replaced by Ivanoe Bonomi as Badoglio was seen as being too close to the Fascist Government.

Fighting in Italy was slow and bitter, with many Italians having to live in terrible conditions with an extortionate black market and widespread corruption. This made Italians less supportive of the Allies. Gradually politics in the south returned to 'normal' – alliances of Catholics, Socialists and Liberals coming together to form a government.

Add the context

Below is a sample exam question with the accompanying sources. Having read the question and the sources, complete the following activity.

> How far could the historian make use of Sources 1 and 2 together to investigate the Italian experiences of Nazi control from 1943 to 1945?

First, look for aspects of the source that refer to the events and discussion that were going on around the time that the source was written. Underline the key phrases and write a brief description of the context in the margin next to the source. Draw an arrow from the key phrase to the context. Try and find three key phrases in each source.

Tip: look at the information above the source – you should contextualise this too. Pay particular attention to the author of the source.

SOURCE 1

From the memoirs of Peter Ghiringhelli. Here, he recalls his experiences of living in the Fascist Republic of Salò, during the later stages of the Second World War.

In 1944, things were really bad and I got used to people being shot or disappearing. The way the Germans now behaved seemed senseless to everybody. The bulk of the Italian army was deported to slave labour in Germany and as civilian young men were rounded up for work in Germany more and more saw joining the partisan bands as the only way of escape. But as more joined them the Nazi and Fascist repression became harsher. This was the year of the Italian civil war, the Partisans against the ultra-Fascist Republicans with very few prisoners taken on either side. Bands of Fascists seemed almost autonomous and clearly out of control with captured partisans having their eyes gauged out or worse before being shot. The area where we lived now was part of the 'Republica Sociale Italiana' (the Italian Social Republic), known as the Republic of Salò, from the small town of Salò on the shores of Lake Garda, where Mussolini now had his headquarters. Ostensibly controlled by Mussolini, the Germans were the real masters.

SOURCE 2

From an appeal to young conscripts by the Italian partisan movement from February 1944.

Italian Brothers ...

The German oppressor and his Neo-Fascist servants want to conscript you in order to make you share in their criminal actions against the liberty and salvation of Italy.

Do not take any notice of their promises.

Do not allow yourself to be taken in by them.

COME

Your brothers the partisans have been fighting for five months for you and they are waiting for you amidst the immaculate snows of the mountains, untouched by the oppressor.

We are waiting for you!

Long live Italy!

Use the context

Having completed the previous activity, read the following statements and work out how to use the context to support the following claims. Write a sentence justifying each of the claims.

Source 1 is correct to argue that 'the Germans were the real masters' of the Republic of Salò because ...

Source 2 is partially valuable to a historian investigating the Italian experiences of Nazi control from 1943 to 1945 because ...

German surrender and Mussolini's death, 1945

REVISED

By 1945, the collapse of fascism and the defeat of German forces in Italy were inevitable. Without the support of German troops the Salò Republic could not survive.

The German surrender

In January 1944, Allied troops landed at Anzio and in May the German Gustav defensive line collapsed. Cassino fell into Allied hands. By April 1945, Germany was on the verge of defeat across Europe and her troops in Italy rapidly retreated to the Austrian border.

At 61 years old, Mussolini lacked the charisma and energy of his early years in power. He was a broken man by this point. Mussolini blamed the Italian population for the failure to achieve the glorious expansion of the Italian empire and the vast majority of Italians were no longer motivated or persuaded by Fascist propaganda. Mussolini hoped a new German miracle would reverse the Allies' military advance. He also hoped that the USA and Britain would turn on the USSR and would need the support of Italy and Germany, but those hopes were completely unrealistic.

On 9 April 1945, the Allies launched a final push into northern Italy. Allied soldiers pushed across the Po Valley in northern Italy in May 1945 and German forces in Italy surrendered on 2 May 1945, two days after the collapse of Berlin.

Mussolini's death

Mussolini tried to leave Italy with an entourage when the Allied advance began, heading for the border to Switzerland on 25 April. Mussolini had no clear plan. He and the German military envoy that was leaving at the same time were stopped by communist partisans near the border, and Mussolini taken prisoner. Mussolini, his mistress and other leading Fascists were executed and their bodies displayed publicly in Milan.

Italian partisans

Partisan resistance groups were active throughout northern and much of central Italy after September 1943. Many were former soldiers cut off from home (including former British, Greek and Slav prisoners of war) and still in possession of their weapons, while others did not want to be conscripted by Mussolini. They specialised in surprise attacks, sabotage, seizure of goods and political assassination. Partisans were fighting three types of war: a civil war against Italian Fascists, a war of national liberation against German occupation and a class war against the ruling elites. The communists led the largest group of partisans, numbering at least 50,000 in 1944, and fought for all these reasons, while Catholic and monarchist partisans had different priorities.

Spectrum of importance

Below is a sample exam question and a list of general points which could be used to answer the question. Use your own knowledge and the information on the opposite page to reach a judgement about the importance of these general points to the question posed. Write numbers on the spectrum below to indicate their relative importance. Having done this, write a brief justification of your placement, explaining why some of these factors are more important than others. The resulting diagram could form the basis of an essay plan.

How significant were divisions within the Fascist Party in bringing about the fall of Mussolini's Fascist regime in 1943?

1 Unpopular foreign policy
2 Defeats during the Second World War
3 Deteriorating conditions during the Second World War
4 Divisions within the Fascist Party
5 Loss of the King's support
6 Allied victory in the Second World War

Less important ←——————————→ Very important

Spot the inference

a

High-level answers avoid excessive summarising or paraphrasing the sources. Instead they make inferences from the sources, as well as analysing their value in terms of their context. Below is a source and a series of statements. Read the source and decide which of the statements:

- make inferences from the source (I)
- paraphrase the source (P)
- summarise the source (S)
- cannot be justified from the source (X).

Statement	I	P	S	X
Mussolini's body was hung upside down from a girder at a petrol station.				
By the time of Mussolini's death, there was little popular support for fascism in Italy				
Following his execution, Mussolini's corpse was displayed in public and large crowds gathered to see it.				
There was significant popular support in Italy for the execution of Mussolini.				
Mussolini was executed by Communist partisans.				
The writer of Source 1 believes that many of the people who had come to see Mussolini's corpse had, in the past, been supporters of Mussolini.				

SOURCE 1

From the diary of Anton Mazzotti, a young journalist from Switzerland. Here he describes seeing the corpses of Mussolini and the other captured Fascists.

While I was away, the 18 corpses had been dragged a few metres further forward. Four of them, including Mussolini, hung by their feet, head down, like butchered animals from a girder above an adjacent petrol station. I was told that this had been done so that those furthest away could see Mussolini. What had once been their shirts now dangled down, leaving the chests of the four white and exposed. The crowd was huge, monstrous and eager, seething and pressing in the immense piazza with a kind of constant, low, indistinct roar. Some people were standing upright on top of the girder as if to act as guards or simply to get sight of such a vast crowd. I was railing – and God knows what I was saying – against everyone, including that foul beast of a crowd that in the past would have rushed to any piazza in Italy to scream deliriously for Mussolini.

The outcomes of the referendum and elections in 1946

REVISED

The Second World War was disastrous for Italy, leading to high unemployment, high cost of living and the loss of nearly all her colonies. Italy's first post-war Government was established in June 1945. It consisted of Socialists, Communists and Christian Democrats, providing a show of unity. After five months a new Government was formed in November 1945. It was dominated by the Christian Democrats, the successors of the Catholic *Popolari*.

The 1946 referendum on the monarchy

After the war, King Victor Emmanuel III was unable to regain his authority and he abdicated in April 1946. The King hoped that his son, Umberto, might revive popular support for the monarchy in time for the referendum on the monarchy in May. However, the Italians voted by 52 per cent to 48 per cent to abolish the Savoy monarchy and establish a republic. Italy therefore became a republic in 1946, but opinion was not evenly spread throughout the country: the north voted mostly for a republic, while the south voted to keep the monarchy. The royal family went into exile and Enrico de Nicola became the provisional head of a new republican state. A new electoral system was introduced, based upon proportional representation.

The elections of 1946

Elections were held for a new 'Constituent Assembly' on the same day as the referendum on the monarchy. For the first time, the electoral franchise was extended to allow women to vote in the election. The election results were interesting: the Christian Democrats, the Catholic heirs to the *Popolari,* won 35.2 per cent of the vote and 207 seats. The Communists won 102 seats, the Socialists 115, the Liberals 41 and the other minor parties made up the rest of the Assembly. The three main parties made up the Government, alongside the new Republican Party, which had 23 seats.

The senate was to be elected, the President was a largely symbolic figure and the Prime Minister was elected mainly by the parliament. Government was to be by a cabinet of ministers which would be responsible to the parliament. This Government was anti-Fascist by construction and definition. It was a weak government that would not be able to repeat the Fascist years.

The Second World War had a horrendous impact on Italy but it paved the way for the collapse of fascism and the emergence of democracy.

Simple essay style

Below are three sample exam questions. Use your own knowledge and the information on the preceding pages to produce plans for these questions. In each case, choose four general points, and provide three pieces of specific information to support each general point. Once you have planned each essay, write the introduction and conclusion for the essay. The introduction should list the points to be discussed in the essay. The conclusion should summarise the key points and justify which point was the most important.

How accurate is it to say that Italian foreign policy became increasingly aggressive in the period 1922–43?

'Mussolini's foreign policy failed to meet its aims in the period 1922–43.' How far do you agree with this statement?

'Fascist Italy failed because Mussolini's foreign policy aims were too ambitious.' How far do you agree with this statement?

Turning assertion into argument

a

Below are a sample exam question and a series of assertions. Read the exam question and then add a justification to each of the assertions to turn it into an argument.

To what extent was the Second World War the main reason for Mussolini's fall from power in 1943?

Deteriorating conditions during the Second World War played an important role in Mussolini's fall from power because ...

____

____

Loss of support from within the Fascist Party played a significant role in Mussolini's fall from power because ...

____

____

Mussolini's foreign policy played a partial role in Mussolini's fall from power because ...

____

____

Recommended reading

- C. Duggan, *Fascist Voices: An Intimate History of Mussolini's Italy*, Chapters 11–13 (2012).
- R. Mallett, *Mussolini and the Origins of the Second World War*, Chapter 1 (2003).
- P. Morgan, *The Fall of Mussolini: Italy, the Italians, and the Second World War* (2007).

Exam focus

REVISED

Below is an exam-style question and high-level model answer. Read it and the comments around it.

To what extent were Mussolini's foreign policy successes responsible for the popularity of the Fascist regime in the years 1922–41?

Mussolini's foreign policy successes, particularly the Abyssinian Campaign, were the main reason for the popularity of the regime in the 1930s. However, Mussolini had few foreign policy successes in the 1920s, and therefore other factors such as the accommodation with the Roman Catholic Church and his campaign against communism are more likely to explain the regime's popularity in the 1920s. Certainly, Mussolini's economic policy contributed little to the popularity of the regime as living standards either stagnated or declined for the majority of Italians in the years 1922–41.

Between 1922 and 1941 Mussolini's foreign policy had two major successes, both of which strengthened the popularity of the Fascist regime. The first was the annexation of Fiume. In March 1923, Mussolini sent Italian troops into the Adriatic port of Fiume. He claimed they were there to stop a revolution. However, in reality he ordered the occupation of Fiume in order to gain control of the area. The policy was a success and Italy's control of Fiume was secured by the Treaty of Rome which Italy signed with Yugoslavia in 1924. This was clearly a success for Mussolini as Italian control of Fiume was a key objective for Italian Nationalists, because it was one of Mussolini's key territorial goals and because the Italian people had shown their support for a takeover of Fiume during D'Annunzio's occupation of Fiume in 1919. This was a major foreign policy success and increased the popularity of the regime soon after it was founded because it allowed Mussolini to claim that fascism had achieved something that Liberal politicians had failed to do in their negotiations over the treaty of Saint-Germain at the end of the First World War, or Giolitti's negotiation over the Treaty of Rapallo in 1920.

> This paragraph shows a detailed knowledge of the annexation of Fiume. It also shows why the policy was a success and analyses why this led to support for the Fascist regime.

Another success was the Abyssinian Campaign of 1935–36. Mussolini's objective was to extend the Italian Empire in Africa by conquering Abyssinia. The campaign started in October 1935. By May 1936, Italian forces, led by Peitro Badoglio, had defeated the forces of Haile Selassie I. Again, this was a success because it achieved Mussolini's objective of extending the Italian Empire. The Italian media also claimed that it demonstrated the excellence of the Italian Army, and the use of 254 aeroplanes, 595 tanks, 30,000 trucks and 4.2 million shells showed Italy's military strength. Additionally, Mussolini refused to back down even when the League of Nations condemned the invasion. Consequently, Mussolini could claim he had beaten not only Abyssinia, but the League of Nations. Therefore, the Abyssinian Campaign, Mussolini's greatest foreign policy success, was clearly responsible for the popularity of the regime because Mussolini had shown he could extend Italy's empire and stand up to the League of Nations.

> This paragraph uses precise detail to support its points.

Other foreign policy successes did not lead to a major increase in the regime's popularity. For example, Italy's involvement in the Spanish Civil War from the middle of 1936 did not lead to increasing popularity. This is because, unlike the Abyssinian Campaign, Italian involvement in the Spanish Civil War did not lead to a quick success or extend the Italian Empire. Equally, Italian involvement in the Second World War from July 1940 did not increase the regime's popularity because the Italian people were not enthusiastic about fighting such a major war, and because by 1941, Italian territorial gains were small. In both cases, these later foreign policy successes were not responsible for the popularity of the Fascist regime because military success did not lead to obvious gains for Italy.

> This paragraph extends the chronological range of the essay to 1941. Consequently, together with the earlier discussion of Fiume, it covers the whole period specified by the question.

However, Mussolini's foreign policy successes were not the only reason for the popularity of the Fascist regime in the years 1922–41. Propaganda and censorship also played a key role. For example, propaganda magnified Italy's successes in the Abyssinian Campaign. Due to propaganda, the Abyssinian Campaign became the high point of the Cult of the Duce. Italian propaganda emphasised the hypocrisy of the imperialist nations such as Britain and France condemning Italy's imperial expansion, and turned Mussolini into an even greater hero in the eyes of the Italian people for standing up to the League of Nations. Censorship, organised by the High Commission, made no reference to the C.L.R. James' campaign through the International African Friends of Ethiopia which was designed to put pressure on Italy to withdraw from Abyssinia. Clearly, Mussolini's foreign policy successes were responsible for the popularity of the Fascist regime in the years 1922–41, but propaganda and censorship played a key role emphasising Mussolini's achievements. Even so, the effects of Fascist propaganda were often quite limited. Indeed, it failed to create mass enthusiasm for Italy's successes in the Spanish Civil War or the early phase of the Second World War. Therefore it would be wrong to overstate the impact of Fascist propaganda.

This paragraph demonstrates high-level skills as it concludes by weighing the relative importance of propaganda and genuine foreign policy successes. However, the answer could have considered some features of domestic propaganda.

Finally, there were clearly other reasons for the popularity of the regime. Fascist corporatism, for example, led to some benefits for workers such as holiday pay and sick pay. A variety of measures persuaded elite groups to back the regime. For example, the Concordat and family policies won the support of the Roman Catholic Church, and radical Fascists such as Aurelio Padovani were sidelined to win over the traditional agricultural elites. Additionally, Fascist propaganda ensured that Mussolini was widely regarded as a strong and decisive leader. In middle class areas propaganda stressed his anti-communism. More generally, the Italian press consistently used various techniques to emphasise his strength. For example, photographers used various techniques to hide Mussolini's short stature (he was 5 ft 5 in), signs of age and to emphasise his physical strength. In this way, foreign policy successes were clearly not the only reason for Fascist popularity in the years 1922–41 because the regime had policies and achievements that won over the major sections of Italian society.

This paragraph demonstrates a breadth of knowledge in very few words. It achieves this by discussing reasons why most major groups in Italian society supported the regime.

In conclusion, Mussolini's foreign policy successes were clearly a big reason for the popularity of the Fascist regime in the years 1922–41. The successes of the Abyssinian Campaign, highlighted by propaganda, clearly led to the high point of the Cult of the Duce and genuine enthusiasm among the Italian people. Moreover, the early success of Fiume was genuinely popular and played a role in the initial consolidation of Fascist rule. Nonetheless, not all of the successes led to popularity. Indeed, only those successes that led to quick territorial gains really made the regime popular. Other aspects of the regime were more important, such as the economic gains made by the working class and the policies, such as the Concordat, which encouraged other important groups to support the regime.

The conclusion makes an overall judgement that reflects the analysis presented in the rest of the essay. However, the assertion that other factors were more important than foreign policy successes is not fully supported.

This is a strong Level 4 answer. It is analytical throughout, and evaluates several different aspects of foreign policy. However, discussion of domestic politics is not extensive, which means that the concluding sentence is not securely supported by detailed evidence.

What makes a good answer?

You have now considered several high-level essays. Use these essays to make bullet-pointed lists of the characteristics of a top-level essay. Use this list when planning and writing your own practice exam essay.

AS-level questions

How successful was the Abyssinian War for Italy?

How far can the Italian involvement in the Second World War be described as a complete disaster?

Glossary

Abyssinia The old name for Ethiopia.

Acerbo Law Mussolini's reform of elections to guarantee a Fascist victory.

Allies The states that opposed the Central Powers in the First World War. These included the Entente Powers, as well as Japan, the USA and Italy.

Autarky Economic independence or self-sufficiency.

Balance of payments deficit A situation in which a nation's imports of goods or services exceeds its exports.

Balkan Wars Two wars, from 1912 to 1913, that were fought for possession of the European territories of the Ottoman Empire (now largely known as Turkey).

Blackshirts Armed Fascist militia.

Central Powers One of the two main factions in the First World War, consisting of Germany, Austria-Hungary, the Ottoman Empire and Bulgaria.

Constitutional monarchy The King was the head of the State but the Prime Minister was the head of the Government. Although the King had the power to dismiss Prime Ministers, in practice day-to-day politics was left in the hands of the Prime Minister and parliament.

Corporate state Under this system every industry would be part of a Fascist-led corporation that would resolve disputes between workers and managements and help to organise production, pay and conditions.

Cult of personality When an individual or state uses propaganda to create an idealised and heroic image of a leader, encouraging unconditional obedience and praise.

Duce Italian for 'leader'. The term, unlike the term 'Prime Minister', was not a constitutional term and therefore implied that there was no constitutional limits on Mussolini's power.

Electoral franchise Those in the population who have the right to vote.

Encyclical A papal letter sent to all the bishops of the Catholic Church.

Entente Powers The allied forces of Great Britain, France and Russia in the First World War.

Grand Council of Fascism The supreme body within the Fascist movement, which discussed policy proposals and made all key appointments within the Fascist Party.

League of Nations An organisation of nations created by the Treaty of Versailles to encourage international co-operation and peace.

Mutilated victory The claim that Italy had been denied its rightful territorial gains in the peace settlement after the First World War.

New industries In the first half of the twentieth century, the term 'new industries' referred to industries that produced relatively high-tech products, such as chemicals and electricity.

OVRA Fascist secret police.

Partisans Armed anti-Fascist groups.

Petty bourgeoisie The lower-middle class, including minor businessmen or traders.

Prefects Powerful local agents of the Fascist Government.

Reparations Compensation to pay for war damage.

Republic of Salò Mussolini's Fascist regime in northern Italy, 1943–35.

Satellite state A country politically and economically dominated or controlled by another more powerful country.

Squadristi Violent Fascist gangs or squads.

Totalitarian A government that attempts to control the lives of its citizens or subjects completely, is dictatorial and demands total obedience.

Trasformismo The technique in Italian Liberal politics of creating a flexible coalition from across the political spectrum, made necessary by the Italian political system.

Universal male suffrage The right of all men to vote.

Key figures

Italo Balbo Joined the National Fascist Party (PNF) when it was founded in 1921. He was an enthusiastic participant and organiser of *squadristi* and later became involved in key developments such as the March on Rome. In 1933 he was appointed Governor-general of Libya. Balbo was the only member of the Fascist regime to oppose legislation against the Jews. He also disagreed with the alliance with Hitler, preferring that Italy ally with Britain instead.

Count Galeazzo Ciano A founding member of the PNF. He married Mussolini's daughter Edda in 1930. Ciano became Minister of Press and Propaganda in 1935 and was appointed Minister of Foreign Affairs in 1936.

Gabriele D'Annunzio An Italian poet, writer and soldier, who became a national hero as an elite officer in the First World War. D'Annunzio, like many Nationalists, was horrified by Italy's 'mutilated victory'. Therefore, in 1919 he led a band of rebel soldiers and took control of Fiume, establishing the Italian Regency of Carnaro. The radical and theatrical nature of D'Annunzio's government of Fiume was a key influence on Mussolini.

Alberto De Stefani Initially a Liberal politician, De Stefani later became a Fascist and gained a seat on the Grand Council of Fascism. He served as Finance Minister from 1922 to 1925. Although De Stefani's policies led to improvements in the Italian economy, he was replaced once the economic momentum began to decrease.

Victor Emmanuel III Became King of Italy in 1900. He supported Italy's entry into the First World War in 1915. The Socialist-organised general strike in July 1922 convinced Victor Emmanuel III that he had to appoint someone who could restore political stability. He felt Mussolini was capable of doing this but did not view his appointment as Prime Minister as a long-term plan. He dismissed Mussolini as Prime Minister in July 1943 following the vote of the Grand Fascist Council and negotiated an armistice with the Allies alongside the new Prime Minister. Victor Emmanuel III abdicated in favour of his son Umberto in 1944, realising he was too closely linked with the Fascist regime.

Roberto Farinacci Was known as one of the most radical Fascists and was involved in organising the *squadristi*. He was important in establishing Fascist dominance in 1922 and became Secretary of the Fascist party in 1925. He urged Mussolini to join with the Axis powers. In 1943, Farinacci colluded with other members of the Grand Council of Fascism to bring about Mussolini's arrest.

Giovanni Giolitti A Liberal politician and five-time Prime Minister of Italy. After Mussolini he is the longest serving Prime Minister in Italian history. Giolitti was an expert in *Trasformismo*, using corruption, patronage and manipulation to achieve his political aims.

Dino Grandi Joined the Blackshirts in 1920 and was elected to the Chamber of Deputies in 1921 alongside 34 other Fascists. He was involved in the March on Rome. Grandi was appointed Minister of Foreign Affairs in 1929. He was always one of the more radical Fascists, supporting violent *squadristi* action. Grandi spearheaded the removal of Mussolini at the Fascist Grand Council in July 1943.

Giacomo Matteotti Opposed the Fascist Party and movement after the First World War. He spoke out in the Chamber of Deputies against the violence used by the Fascists during the 1924 elections. Matteotti was subsequently kidnapped and murdered, his body being found in a shallow grave 23 kilometres from Rome. His murder led to increased criticism of fascism and of Mussolini.

Benito Mussolini Fascist dictator of Italy from 1925 to 1943. He was initially a radical socialist, but became increasingly convinced that nationalism was the key to political power. Having supported Italy's participation in the First World War and considered a communist revolution in Italy, Mussolini joined the Fascists. He became Prime Minister in 1922 and established a dictatorship by the end of 1925.

Timeline

1861 Establishment of the Kingdom of Italy

1892 Italian Socialist Party (PSI) established

1896 Italian army defeated at Adowa

1903 Giolitti becomes Prime Minister

1910 Italian Nationalist Association founded

1911 Beginning of the Libyan War

1912 Franchise extended to all literate men over 21 and all men over 30

1914 Resignation of Giolitti

1915 Treaty of London

1919 Widespread industrial unrest

Creation of the Catholic Popular Party

Fasci di Combattimento launched

Invasion of Fiume by Italian Nationalists

1921 Italian Communist Party founded

National Fascist Party founded

1922 March on Rome

Mussolini becomes Prime Minister

Mussolini granted emergency powers

Grand Council of Fascism created

1923 Acerbo Law passed

1924 Annexation of Fiume

General election: Fascists gain two-thirds of the seats in new parliament

Matteotti Crisis

1925 Battle for Grain introduced

Locarno Pact signed

Mussolini given the title *Duce*

1926 *Opera Nazionale Balilla* (ONB) established

Strikes banned

Battle for the Lira introduced

All political parties except the Fascist Party banned

OVRA secret police established

All opposition newspapers closed

1927 Battle for Births policy introduced

1928 Kellogg–Briand Pact

1929 Concordat signed with the Pope

1931 Homosexuality banned

1935 Policy of autarky adopted

1936 Start of the Spanish Civil War

Italian invasion of Abyssinia

1937 Italy signs the Anti-Comintern Pact

1939 Pact of Steel established

1940 Italy enters the Second World War

1943 Mussolini sacked as Prime Minister and arrested

Mussolini becomes head of the Salò Republic

1945 Mussolini killed by Italian Communist guerrillas

1946 Italy declared a republic after a referendum

Mark schemes

Paper 2 requires two mark schemes, one for the AO2 assessments in Section A and another for Section B's AO1 assessment.

AO1 mark scheme:

- Analytical focus
- Accurate detail
- Supported judgement
- Argument and structure

Level	Marks	Description
1	1–3	• Simplistic statements. • Very limited accurate and relevant knowledge. • There is either no overall judgement, or it is very basic. • Very little structure or argument.
2	4–7	• Descriptive statements about key features. • Mostly accurate and relevant knowledge, but limited in terms of range and depth. • An overall judgement is presented, but with limited support. The judgement lacks clear criteria. • The work shows the beginnings of structure and a limited attempt to create an argument.
3	8–12	• Some analysis of key features. • Mostly accurate and relevant knowledge, is used in a way that shows some understanding of the question. The range and depth may be limited in places. • An overall judgement is presented. It is supported with an attempt to establish criteria. • Some structure and a generally clear argument.
4	13–16	• Analysis of key features. • Sufficient accurate and relevant knowledge is used to answer most aspects of the question. • An overall judgement is presented. It is based on valid criteria, but may only be partially supported. • A well-structured essay with a clear argument, although in places the argument may lack precision.
5	17–20	• Sustained analysis of key features. • Sufficient accurate and relevant knowledge is used to answer all key aspects of the question. • An overall judgement is presented. It is based on valid criteria and is fully supported. The relative significance of the criteria may be considered while reaching the judgement. • A well-structured essay with a clear argument which is communicated with precision.

AO2 mark scheme:

- Analytical focus
- Accurate detail
- Supported judgement

Level	Marks	Description
1	1–3	• Surface level comprehension of the sources, demonstrated by quoting or paraphrasing, without analysis. • Some relevant knowledge of the historical context is included, but links to the sources are limited. • There is either no overall evaluation of the sources, or discussion of reliability and utility is very basic.
2	4–7	• Some understanding of the sources, demonstrated by selecting and summarising relevant information. • Some relevant knowledge of the historical context is linked to the extracts to support or challenge the detail they include. • An overall judgement is presented, but with limited support. Discussion of reliability and utility are based on a limited discussion of provenance and may reflect invalid assumptions.
3	8–12	• Understanding of the sources, demonstrated by some analysis of key points, explaining their meaning and valid inferences. • Relevant knowledge of the historical context is used to support inferences. Contextual knowledge is also used to expand on, support or challenge matters of detail. • An overall judgement is presented, which relates to the nature and purpose of the sources. The judgement is based on valid criteria, but the support is likely to be limited.
4	13–16	• Analysis of the sources, demonstrated by examining their evidence to make reasoned inferences. Valid distinctions are made between information and opinion. Treatment of the two sources may be uneven. • Relevant knowledge of the historical context is used to reveal and discuss the limitations of sources' content. The answer attempts to interpret the source material in the context of the values and assumptions of the society it comes from. • An overall judgement regarding the interpretation is presented which is supported by valid criteria. Evaluation of the sources reflects how much weight the evidence of the sources can bear. Aspects of the judgement may have limited support.
5	17–20	• Confident interrogation of both sources demonstrated by reasoned inferences. The answer shows a range of ways the sources can be used, making valid distinctions between information and opinion. • Relevant knowledge of the historical context is used to reveal and discuss the limitations of the sources' content. The answer interprets the source material in the context of the values and assumptions of the society it comes from. • An overall judgement regarding the interpretation is presented which is supported by valid criteria. Evaluation of the sources reflects how much weight the evidence of the sources can bear and may distinguish between the degrees to which aspects of the sources can be useful.

Answers

Page 9, Develop the detail – suggested answer

Economic problems played some role in creating social discontent in Italy in the period 1911–18. Although many in the north benefited from industrial growth, southern workers suffered in this period. For example, Nitti's attempts to modernise southern industry were largely unsuccessful. **He ended internal tariffs and introduced free trade, but these measures just damaged the southern economy.** In addition, there were significant problems with agriculture in the south. **The land was of low quality, and deforestation, coupled with a series of droughts, reduced agricultural productivity.** As a result of these problems, the south was significantly less wealthy than the north, **having only 27 per cent of the nation's wealth, compared with 48 per cent in the north.** In this way, economic problems contributed to social discontent in Italy in the period 1911–18 because they decreased standards of living for those in the south and accentuated the divide between the south and the north.

Page 11, Spot the mistake

The answer is focused, but does not contain sufficient detail to be awarded a mark in Level 4.

Page 11, Spot the inference

There was significant social and economic turmoil in Italy in this period. **S**

The writer of Source 1 believes that Giolitti's Government tried to make life easier for the poor. **X**

The writer of Source 1 believes that Italian governments in the period described did not deal effectively with the social and economic problems facing Italy. **I**

There were protests among labourers and peasants and those in the south. **P**

The writer of Source 1 believes that the main cause of social discontent was bad harvests. **X**

The writer of Source 1 believes that economic problems were a significant cause of social discontent. **I**

Politically, there were many twists and turns in Italy before the First World War. **P**

Page 13, Write the question – suggested answer

Why is Source 1 valuable to the historian for an enquiry into the success of the Liberal regime in Italy in the period 1911–14?

Page 21, Identify the concept

How far did the lives of poor Italians change in the period 1911–18? (AS question) – **change/continuity**

'The First World War had only negative consequences for the people of Italy.' How far do you agree? – **consequence**

'The Liberal State transformed Italy in the period 1911–18.' How far do you agree? – **change/continuity**

How far was dislike of *Trasformismo* the most important factor in Italy's political changes from 1911 to 1914? (AS question) – **cause**

'The most important cause of the fall of Giolitti was the war in Libya.' How far do you agree with this statement? – **cause**

How far was the signing of the Treaty of London the most important turning point in the intervention crisis of 1914–15? – **significance**

Page 27, Identify an argument

Sample 1 contains the argument.

Page 27, Eliminate irrelevance

The invasion of Fiume in September 1919 played a key role in undermining the Liberal State in the years 1918–22. In this respect, the invasion was significant for three reasons. Firstly, the invasion showed the lack of support for the Government among the military. The invasion, which involved two thousand soldiers, occurred in defiance of the Liberal Government, and indicated that many in the military were not loyal to the Government. ~~**This had also been a problem in 1916, when many soldiers had expressed discontent at Italy's Government during the war.**~~ Secondly, the invasion showed the lack of popular support for the Liberal Government. Many in Italy supported the invasion, and viewed D'Annunzio as a hero. ~~**D'Annunzio was also famous for being a poet.**~~ Thirdly, the invasion demonstrated the power of force, undermining the Liberal State's reliance on compromise and negotiation. In this way, the invasion of Fiume contributed to the political instability of the Liberal State in the years 1918–22 by emphasising the level of popular dissatisfaction with the Liberal Government and its methods.

Page 29, Spot the inference

The gangs in Italy carried out pickpocketing, abuse, robberies and murders. **P**

Italian workers were frustrated because they felt they were working too many hours. **X**

The Government in Italy did not deal effectively with the economic and social crisis in this period. **I**

The writer believes that the social and economic crisis in Italy had the potential to lead to the establishment of a Communist regime in Italy. **S**

The Communists did not come to power in Italy. Instead, a Fascist regime took the place of the Liberal State. **I**

Nationalist pride was an important factor in the rise of fascism in Italy. **I**

The economic crisis in Italy was worse in the south because economic conditions were worse in that region. **X**

If Italy had fallen to the Communists, other countries would have laughed and joked about it. **P**

Page 31, Write the question – suggested answer

How far could the historian make use of Sources 1 and 2 together to investigate **the reasons for the economic and political crisis in Italy in the years 1919–22?**

or

How far could the historian make use of Sources 1 and 2 together to investigate **the reasons for the appeal of fascism in Italy in the period 1919–22?**

Page 33, Use the context – suggested answers

Source 1 is correct to suggest that the 'mass of the workers' did not support Fascist violence because **much Fascist violence targeted Socialists, and many workers were supporters of the Socialist Party.**

Source 2's description of the influence of the Socialist Party as 'the red terror' reflects the writer's political position because**, as a Fascist, Balbo viewed the Socialists as a threat to Italy.**

The fact that Source 1 and Source 2 provide similar accounts of the nature of Fascist violence in this period makes them more valuable to a historian because **the authors of Source 1 and Source 2 have different political opinions, and might, therefore, be expected to view the violence differently. For example, we might expect the author of Source 2 – a Fascist – to give a more positive account of the actions of the Fascist squads. The fact that both the author of Source 1 – a Liberal – and the author of Source 2 agree that the violence was preceded by threats, focused on workers' organisations, and led to widespread destruction adds credibility to their accounts.**

Page 45, Identify the concept

How far were the elections of 1919 the most important turning point in the collapse of the Liberal State in Italy? – **significance**

How far do you agree that the consolidation of Fascist power in the years 1922–28 was mainly due to the use of terror and violence? – **cause**

'The Fascist movement in 1926 was unrecognisable from its beginnings in 1919.' How far do you agree with this statement? **– change/continuity**

How accurate is it to say that the Italian Liberal State was responsible for its own downfall? – **cause**

How far did Mussolini transform the Italian political system in the period 1922–28? – **change/continuity**

Page 51, Develop the detail – suggested answer

Propaganda played an important role in establishing and maintaining Fascist control over Italy in the period 1925–40. The Cult of *Il Duce* was used to suggest that Mussolini was a heroic leader. **He was portrayed as strong and energetic, with no weaknesses.** In addition, the media was used to promote Fascist propaganda. Film production and screening was regulated. **For example, in 1934, the General Directorate of Cinema was created to ensure that films shown in Italy upheld Fascist values.** Furthermore, radio broadcasts were used to spread Fascist propaganda. **In 1933, a radio agency, the ERR, was set up, and Mussolini ensured that over 2 million radios were installed in public places**. Radio broadcasts were an effective means of spreading propaganda **because they allowed Fascist propaganda to reach those who were not literate**. Mussolini also controlled the press. **He introduced measures to control appointments of journalists and the content of the newspapers.** In this way, propaganda was used to establish and maintain Fascist control of Italy in the period 1925–40 by encouraging people to see Mussolini as strong and dynamic and by exercising tight control over film, radio and newspaper production.

Page 55, Complete the paragraph – suggested answer

The Fascist State had the support of the Italian monarchy to a fair extent. On the one hand, the King showed his support for the Fascist State as he signed the majority of Mussolini's decrees. In addition, he did not challenge a reduction in his own power. For example, he accepted that Mussolini did not seek his advice on policy making, and he agreed that the power to decide who succeeded to the Italian throne should be passed to the Fascist Grand Council. Furthermore, he did not try to use the army to restrict the power of the Fascist State. However, the King did resist some elements of fascism. For example, he refused to incorporate the Fascist symbol into the Italian flag, and he criticised Fascist anti-Semitic policy. **In this way, while the King did not completely support the Fascist State, he did little to oppose it.**

Page 57, Spot the inference

Mussolini called for illegal activities to end for there to be no more violence. **P**

Mussolini believed that the actions of the *squadrismo* could undermine his power and it should be disbanded. **I**

The Prefect represented the central government. **P**

Mussolini's system of government was inefficient. **X**

Fascist prefects had significant amounts of power. **I**

Mussolini sought to centralise power in Italy. **I**

Page 59, Write the question – suggested answer

How far could the historian make use of Sources 1 and 2 together to investigate **Mussolini's motives for creating the corporate state?**

Page 73, Identify an argument

Sample 1 includes an argument.

Page 77, Write the question – suggested answer

How far could the historian make use of Sources 1 and 2 together to investigate **the reaction of the Italian population to the invasion of Abyssinia in 1935?**

Page 79, You're the examiner

Level 2 – Descriptive statements about some key features of Mussolini's foreign policy. Focus on the question is weak.

Page 83, Develop the detail – suggested answer

Italian military weaknesses during the Second World War played a significant role in bringing about the collapse of fascism in Italy. For example, Mussolini insisted on being involved in key decision making. **This was disastrous as he had only a limited grasp of warfare and no coherent strategy.** In addition, the weapons provided were inadequate. **Problems with the supply of weapons meant that only half of Italian units were armed, and many soldiers were forced to use similar weapons to those used in the First World War.** Finally, training of soldiers was inadequate. **Military academies were old-fashioned and consequently many officers were not trained in modern warfare techniques.** In this way, Italian military weaknesses during the Second World War played a significant role in bringing about the collapse of fascism in Italy because soldiers felt let down by Mussolini and his Government, and sought an alternative.

Page 85, Identify the concept

How accurate is it to say that Italian foreign policy became increasingly aggressive in the period 1922–43? – **change/continuity**

To what extent was Mussolini's foreign policy successful in the period 1922–29? – **consequence**

'Fascist Italy failed because Mussolini's foreign policy aims were too ambitious.' How far do you agree with this statement? – **cause**

How accurate is it to say that public dissent played a fundamental role in the collapse of fascism in Italy in 1943? **– significance**

How far can the Italian involvement in the Second World War be described as a complete disaster? **– consequence**

Page 91, Spot the inference

Mussolini's body was hung upside down from a girder at a petrol station. **P**

By the time of Mussolini's death, there was little popular support for fascism in Italy. **I**

Following his execution, Mussolini's corpse was displayed in public and large crowds gathered to see it. **S**

There was significant popular support in Italy for the execution of Mussolini. **I**

Mussolini was executed by Communist partisans. **X**

The writer of Source 1 believes that many of the people who had come to see Mussolini's corpse had, in the past, been supporters of Mussolini. **I**

Page 93, Turning assertion into argument – suggested answer

Deteriorating conditions during the Second World War played an important role in Mussolini's fall from power because **public opinion turned against Mussolini, leading to the growth of organised opposition to the regime.**

Loss of support from within the Fascist Party played a significant role in Mussolini's fall from power because **it showed that those who had previously been most loyal to him had lost confidence in his leadership.**

Mussolini's foreign policy played a partial role in Mussolini's fall from power because **although early foreign policy successes boosted Mussolini's popularity, his later policy was much less successful and played a key role in reducing popular and political support for the regime.**